THANATOPICS

THANATOPICS

Activities and Exercises for Confronting Death

J. EUGENE KNOTT
MARY C. RIBAR
BETTY M. DUSON
MARC R. KING

Lexington Books
D.C. Heath and Company
Lexington, Massachusetts/Toronto

Excerpt from *You Are Not the Target* by Laura Archera Huxley. Copyright © 1963 by Laura Huxley. Reprinted by permission of Farrar, Straus and Giroux, Inc.

Library of Congress Cataloging-in-Publication Data

Thanatopics : activities and exercises for confronting
  death.

  Includes index.
  1. Thanatology. I. Knott, J. Eugene.
HQ1073.T535   1989   306'.9   88–36402
ISBN 0–669–20871–X (alk. paper)

Published simultaneously in Canada
Printed in the United States of America
International Standard Book Number: 0–669–20871–X
Library of Congress Catalog Card Number 88–36402

The paper used in this publication meets the minimum requirements of
American National Standard for Information Sciences—Permanence of
Paper for Printed Library Materials, ANSI Z39.48–1984.

∞™

89 90 91 92 8 7 6 5 4 3 2 1

Contents

Acknowledgments

SIGNIFICANT contributions that are intact or only slightly modified from the first edition of this manual are gratefully acknowledged as having come from John Bonaguro, Bob Fulton, Pat Hess, Bob Kastenbaum, Russell Kolton, Earl Knott, Joan McNeil, Greg Owen, Panna Rothe, Mike Slavit, Dorothy Stanton, Steve Steele, Dorree Waldbaum, and Susan Woolsey.

Suggestions and encouragement for this edition are acknowledged with gratitude also to Terrie Rando and to our many other colleagues and students who have offered suggestions for improvements we might make in the activities and book.

Gratitude, too, goes to our editor at Lexington Books, Margaret Zusky, whose initial enthusiasm about and receptivity to a second edition made it happen and whose valuable critique helped render the final product in its current form and substance.

Introduction

Background

W. Somerset Maugham, the famous British writer who was also a physician, reportedly uttered these final words as he lay dying nearly twenty–five years ago: "Dying is a very dull, dreary affair. And my advice to you is to have nothing whatever to do with it" (Brandeth 1979). Maugham's admonishment notwithstanding, none of us can avoid involvement with death and dying numerous times in out lives. And not many these days would regard it as a dull affair, especially in survivorship. Today the very public figures that modern media make of dying celebrities and of victims of spectacular or mass death necessarily involve us strongly and often. Feifel (1977) has put it still another way: "Death is the greatest democracy of all, and we shall all be observer-participants in it" (p. 5).

Yet as Killilea (1988) points out so eloquently, our private and public regards for death and dying today are perhaps best characterized as living with paradox. We sound and behave frequently in seeming contradictions of any consistent belief system about mortality. We sorely need individual and collective efforts at resolving these paradoxes.

Learning about our relationships with mortality, loss, and bereavement in advance of being grief stricken or moribound might accomplish that by serving well these three basic purposes:

1. Aiding us in clarifying our beliefs, feelings, and behaviors about what matters in our lives while we are still vital.
2. Providing at least a modicum of realistic expectation about controlability, quality, and finality across the life span.

3. Enabling dialogue about the legacies to be left and the increasingly difficult decisions to be made in the face of dying in this era of medical technocracy.

Such objectives as these are not readily gained through the mere dispensation of information, for they encompass personal values, self-image, life goals, coping styles, relationships, and philosophy about the tenor and length of living.

Death education has come to be a pervasive reality in the United States, particularly since the late 1970s. Certainly in formal education, it has become an increasingly notable curricular element, from lower grade levels on through a broad range of professional training settings (Pine 1986; Dickinson, Sumner, and Durand 1987; Morgan 1987; Wass, Berardo, and Neimeyer 1988). Nondegree learners too have found frequent, even regular opportunities for personal inspection and exchange of knowledge, beliefs, and skills about human mortality. From community agencies, religious groups, hospice programs, funeral establishments, and a number of other sponsors, death education has become a nearly fixed part of the contemporary scene. Common to all these efforts are three overarching objectives: information sharing, value clarification, and inculcation of coping behaviors (Knott 1979).

Purpose

This book is designed to provide educators and learners with a variety of structured exercises and organized discussion activities that will assist them in examining and integrating the often confused or elusive feelings and attitudes they have toward death. This book is a highly complementary resource for death educators of all stripes but particularly those from middle school through higher and professional education and hospice, agency, community, and religious instructors dealing with the topics presented in this book.

Thanatopics is arranged in a highly usable form, emphasizing the intact character of each learning activity, yet organized into a handful of sections with internal consistency and thematic relatedness. The exercises are written in a fashion that enables a total learning experience, not a discrete, reflexive format that can abuse learner, topic, and instructor alike. All structured learning experiences (SLEs) are multiply tested, later generation revisions, having benefited from many reiterative trials and improvements. Our experience has consistently reinforced both Durlak's (1978) and Oshman's (1978) findings regarding the desirable and superior effects of experiential methods of learning, specifically about death and dying.

Following the appearance of the first edition of this manual in 1982, scores of instructors from many arenas of death education kindly let us know what a helpful tool these structured learning activities are in their efforts. We are particularly gratified by the breadth of age and developmental level and the diversity of purposes to which these exercises have been addressed. This second edition has been revised and updated, and a sizable number of new materials and SLEs have been incorporated. Although the format is essentially unchanged, nearly 40 percent of the content is substantially rewritten or entirely new, reflecting emerging issues or changing perspectives in the field and society at large.

Why This Approach?

Several reasons support this structured experiential approach to death education. The more compelling are these:

1. *Most people need structure to assist them in exploring and discussing death-related issues.* Structure offers both encouragement and relative safety to examine feelings and thoughts that normally are defended against by an individual left to his or her solitary devices. This would appear to be so especially in this era of Westernized living, where death for most is once removed from frequent personal acquaintance by the institutionalization of dying. Adding to this effect is the buffering or insulating from reality that portrayals of death in modern media often promote when they emphasize solely the sensational aspects. The use of structure in group activities has come to be recognized as a valuable and widely employed psychoeducational tool since the mid-1970s (Drum and Lawler 1988).

2. *Effective death education is tied closely to the interpersonal context in which it occurs.* New learning experiences are often enriched when integrated through constructive interaction with others. This seems particularly relevant to a topic like death, which is subject to individual and situational vagaries. By exposing oneself simultaneously to other's views and to one's own inner thoughts and feelings about personal mortality and loss, there often occurs a mutually facilitative process of combined subjective and objective learning.

   In an excellent discussion on many of the issues of importance in experiential group education, Marks and Davis (1975) point out well the merits of the experiential approach over a merely didactic one. They compare the former to participating in a lively discussion, while the latter contrasts sharply as listening to a one-way lecture. The differences are drawn between the two, particularly on the issues of involvement and responsibility. In the experiential model, one becomes involved in a process of active learning, while the didactic is limited to activity on the part of the lecturer, aside from any intellectual stimulation the listener gains. They go on to argue that the entire frame of reference one assumes in experiential learning is more learner centered and can incorporate greater numbers economically while expanding the potential diversity of views. In sum, they point out, such a model is more complete, allowing for personal points of reference, both cognitive and affective exchanges, and incorporation of theoretical or conceptual material. Generally the transfer of learning beyond the initial experience is usually found to be greater and more lasting as well.

3. *Learning about death is a lifelong process.* Experiential education in a group context maximizes the likelihood of continued learning throughout one's developmental passages. This can occur through early removal of impediments to exploration, teaching a process of seeking, and by modeling the value of plain, straight talk about death and dying, their implications and meanings. Developmental researchers have argued that the experience of loss and life-threatening challenges are part of the human legacy and occur regularly throughout life (Viorst 1986). As one matures and life changes are experienced, including losses of significant others, the perspective one acquires with each transitional shift brings with it a concurrent alteration in viewpoint and even behavioral change, as the specter of mortality is renewed and becomes personal in its implications. As LaGrand (1988) put it, "expected and unexpected losses, especially death, shape the character and skills by which survivors live. Renewed moral strength is a by-product of adversity and the willingness to use death as part of the life-long *growth* process" (p. 29).

Structured group exercises have been strongly advocated as a productive way of enabling one to confront the existential meanings of personal death. While our first and most common lessons in this vein are usually unstaged, natural occurrences, those who teach about these topics must also assist learners in integrating and crystallizing the import of those changes and transitions.

Conducting SLEs

There are a number of important points for consideration for leaders of SLEs. These concerns are relevant to the implementation of these activities and to the design of any new ones. We'll begin with some general issues and then move to a more detailed look at the specifics of facilitation and the format of this book.

Facilitation Issues

The leader who is conducting an SLE must do more than simply follow a step-by-step guide. Facilitating an SLE is more complex than merely rendering a recipe. The facilitator must attend with equal skill to what is done, as well as how it comes about. Therein lies the ultimate responsibility and the true process of learning in an experiential mode:

to begin acquiring a new understanding of oneself as a result of a novel and personalized experience.

We encourage the leader to attend to a four-step pattern of usage when employing these activities:

1. **Preparation.** The leader should gather needed materials, become familiar with background topical information, attend to the timing of the activity in the broader scheme of instruction, and review the exercise, preferably by walking through components.
2. **Goal setting.** A critical stage setting by adapting the SLE's goals to the learners and their objectives is accomplished by a clear, concise introduction at the outset, outlining the learning goals for the activity.
3. **Facilitation.** Effective conduct of the SLE demands familiarity with the procedures and any variants to be used while simultaneously attending to the pace, group dynamics, and the often necessary ad hoc modifications that arise due to unexpected reactions.
4. **Processing.** This is the crux of the SLE, where analysis and synthesis can occur best. As Corr and Corr (1982) note:

> *Our enduring conviction with regard to death-related exercises is that in the end it is the* process *which really counts, not the ostensive results. What such exercises actually do is help to initiate a process of personal exploration or to extend a self-reflective inquiry. That process is particularly valuable in a culture where it has too often been avoided or discouraged.* (p. 11).

The SLE should end with a summary that incorporates the goal statements made earlier and assesses the activities' effects on learners.

Facilitator Functions

Yalom (1985) has written about four basic functions that accrue to the group facilitator. He speaks first of the *emotional stimulator*, especially crucial with the often emotive nature of death-related topics. This skill demands a balance between being evocative and yet keeping the process at a level that allows optimal learning and managing intensity to maximize involvement, not simply to stimulate and leave members to their own wits in coping with the emotions stirred.

He writes, too, of the need for *caring*—for not regarding participants as actors in a play or subjects in an experiment but being responsible for the human enterprise that SLEs are. No less than fully attentive, compassionate concern is demanded of group leaders.

Vital to the group's outcomes is the function referred to as *meaning attribution*—the ability to make beneficial, educative use of the SLE. This is perhaps the most important function; the lessons come home only with a skilled facilitator who can enable others to analyze their own experience and mesh that of others into a meaningful viewpoint. No small part of this is seeing that all vantage points are given wider view so that all are appreciated and weighed, particularly as variance and diversity emerge.

Finally, the so-called *executive function* or managerial aspect of leadership is described. This calls for a thorough working knowledge of the logistics of the activity, execution of the procedures with accuracy and timing, and responsible control of the process.

To summarize with a checklist for facilitators, let's consider the following five premises as essential to effective facilitation of SLEs. In brief, they are, *familiarity* with:

1. The *topic* being addressed in the exercise.
2. The *audience* being led through the SLE.
3. The various elements of *group dynamics.*
4. The specific *activities* to be carried out.
5. The *resources* available for assisting with reactions to the exercise.

This last item bears some elaboration. It is inevitable that over time, in using SLEs with this topic, a leader will encounter a participant overidentifying and having a rough time with the feelings elicited. For instance, a member of a learning group may be a recently bereaved person for whom the activity may trigger some painful memories, thoughts, and feelings. The facilitator must be able to help the person cope with this unexpected reaction. Sometimes this will also mean seeking a referral for additional support and counseling help later on. This part of a thorough preparation and delivery may not be needed often, but it is important; leaders must learn to anticipate the unplanned and be adaptable to the situation.

Introducing and Carrying out the Activity

Participation

At the outset of any SLE, each participant should be made fully aware that the level of involvement they choose is a personal decision. While risk taking is to be encouraged, no one should feel coerced in any way to become involved. By modeling such acceptance and flexibility, the facilitator is the key figure in establishing the kind of open, permissive atmosphere that legitimizes voluntary participation and thereby steers clear of unethical conduct.

Developmental Sequencing

Because of the nature and variety of the SLEs in this manual, some will involve deeper levels of exploration and disclosure than others. Some are intended to be introductory, while others are suitable only for a group with a cohesive cohistory. Also although most SLEs are aimed at adult learners, they are also readily adaptable to as young as middle school level. Facilitators should pay attention to providing a SLE attuned to the readiness levels of the audience.

Timing

The temporal feet on which SLEs move are a true pair. Timing is a matter of knowing what to use and when in order to achieve the desired result. This is the "pivot foot." The other foot is the more mobile one, consisting mainly of a flexible length for the activity, with adequate time for debriefing and follow-up being the most critical allowance.

Physical Logistics

The location or setting can be an important feature. Portable seating is usually desired to afford flexibility in subgrouping. Comfort in the surroundings is a key facet of the arrangements; too austere or intemperate an environment is distracting and can compromise the impact of the SLE needlessly. Materials and media aids are important. Two thoughts seem fitting here: complexity demands simplification for most to grasp it, and examples tell twice as well. Overuse of such aids is also to be avoided; careful planning and moderation are the cornerstones of good planning.

Debriefing

Processing by exploration and discussion of the experience and its impacts is essential to experiential learning. Facilitators should ensure adequate time for talking about the feelings, thoughts, and actions generated by a particular SLE. By talking, participants are assisted in clarifying, refining, and extending their learning so that appropriate generalizations and personal messages might be extracted from a given design.

   Several additional guidelines are suggested for ensuring optimal usage of the debriefing procedures:

1. While respecting each one's right to privacy and silence, the leader must obtain a comprehensive view of the reactions and effects the SLE had on different learners.
2. Discovery of interaction patterns and the evolution of group cohesion can be facilitated best through discussion of commonalities and contrasting experiences.
3. Individual differences in response to the exercise are always to be valued. Legitimizing a variety of reactions and realizations about the topic may also be furthered by integrated reference to the goals as they are highlighted in the debriefing.

   SLEs are powerful interventions and teaching tools. They should be utilized with care and the wisdom of moderation that comes with growing experience with this general topic and with different SLEs and various groups.

Completion of SLEs

Like any other intervention, SLEs demand evaluation of their overall effects on learners, including use of immediate participant feedback and later critique. Despite these being well-tested, frequently revised versions of their predecessors, evaluation always has a place in quality experiential education.

Innovation

The outlines to follow must be viewed as somewhat general guidelines. The need to experiment, innovate, and personalize is nowhere greater than with this topic and this methodology. What is presented here are sets of central ideas, with the schemata for application and variation provided.

Learner Responsibility

SLEs build on personal inference, on an active, inductive learning paradigm, as opposed to the basically deductive or reductionistic bases of more impersonal bodies of knowledge. The primary responsibility for learning rests with the participant-learner and endorses the belief that personal learning is preceded by acquisition of new experience, new "data," both intellectual and affective.

Augmenting the SLE

The use of brief lectures to support, expand, or to translate from personal meaning to general application is a worthwhile means of augmenting SLEs. Conceptual material in combination with experiential learning molds a process of education that enables one to integrate both cognitive and conative aspects.

Although the outcomes of structured group learning are sometimes felt to be therapeutic experiences, that end is clearly secondary. The structure is devised to promote an educational character, not one of therapy.

There are over a hundred hours of activities in the pages that follow. Some of the uses and advantages of these singly or in combination include:

- Ability to choose an SLE to fit the particular needs of the learning group or class.
- Selection from several related themes and topically appropriate exercises.
- Clearly spelled out objectives and goals for each activity.
- A common format throughout for ease of use and comparative analysis of experience or theme.
- Frequent explicit narrative suggestions for facile use.
- A readable and adaptable style with easy indexing of related topics and types of activities.

Categories of SLEs Each of the exercises is grouped into one of six major categories. This system is totally of our choosing, and we hope readers will be stimulated to improve on and expand the usage of the ideas to other applications in death education.

1. *Warm-ups and Icebreakers:* Fairly superficial in their impact, these are intended to help broach the topic at hand while offering a fairly high degree of psychological safety. They are best used early in the life of a group, course, workshop, or program to introduce participants to one another and to the salient topics.

2. *Instrumental Exercises and Applied Designs:* This chapter presents a short collection of forms—some newly devised, some generally available in similar format. All require written involvement, usually beginning individually and then moving to group interaction. They allow the flexibility of successive sessions and combine self-exploration and decision-making rehearsal.

3. *Values Clarification and Affective Experiences:* Sid Simon, the father of this form of learning, suggested that death issues provide the ultimate value clarification experience. This category contains some reasonably intense, self-disclosive SLEs whose purpose is to illuminate personal postures toward some aspect of mortality. They should not be employed in an initial meeting or with a group unfamiliar with one another.

4. *Role Plays:* This chapter contains a series of vignettes designed to elicit new perspectives through enactment of a role. While there are few limits to the ways one might employ these, not all are readily able to glean value from the portrayals, often due to poor role playing. This can be a dynamic mode of learning, but care and skill in both acting and debriefing can make or break the outcome here.

4.1 These short two- and three-person role-play vignettes offer the beginning of dialogue for role-playing brief exchanges having to do with issues of loss, separation, dying, and death. They extend the previous chapter's general thrust, but all in this section are simple initial dialogues for illuminating and personalizing the issues presented. Included are suggestions for role-players. Facilitators and instructors are encouraged to use these as the beginnings of presentations and dialogues that can be elaborated on with ease and flexibility.

4.2 There is a second level of role play situations in this edition. They were added to extend the approach into the more complex scenarios and problematic issues that have become our societal legacy in recent years. All are based on actual events and involve a more extensive portrayal of several sticky and important issues.

5. *Artistic Considerations:* New also to *Thanatopics* this time is a brief segment addressing the many extant forms of expressive art and media that are available for helping one confront mortality.

This section offers a generic approach with the common SLE format and a lengthy set of questions to choose from for debriefing. The arts provide us with some of the best learning opportunities in this topic area.

6. *Multisession SLE:* A final addition to this version of the book is a ten-hour structured group format for helping the bereaved make further progress with their mourning. It offers a useful, extensively tested format for assisting people to cope with their grief experience.

Format of SLEs

Below is a short explanation of each component of the SLE format used in this compilation of exercises. They appear in the order found in each exercise:

Title: The label given as a working description of the topical focus of the SLE.

Goals: The broad objectives of the total experience outlined.

Materials and Setting: The tools and quantities of them needed, along with any variables desired for the physical setting.

Time: The overall minimum required to conduct the SLE.

Procedures: A step-by-step outline of each part of the SLE, including leader notes and narrative as applicable.

Variations: Alternative ideas for achieving comparable results; procedural options are frequently offered.

Debriefing: Suggestions for framing the process of inquiry into the effects of the experience on participants, the processing phase that completes each SLE.

The Adventures Begin

We hope your use of the materials that follow will lead to the kinds of enlightening, productive, and enjoyable learning experiences we have had with these SLEs. We encourage and welcome your feedback about your adventures in learning and leading SLEs. Please write us in care of the publisher, Lexington Books, at 125 Spring Street, Lexington, Massachusetts, 02173.

References

Brandreth, G. 1979. *871 Famous last words.* New York: Bell Publishing, 49.

Corr, C.A., and Corr, D.M. 1982. "Exercises about death: Facts, fiction, and values." Paper presented at National Hospice Organization Conference, St. Louis.

Dickinson, G.E.; Sumner, E.D.; and Durand, R.P. 1987. Death education in U.S. professional colleges: Medical, nursing, and pharmacy. *Death Studies* 11:57–61.

Drum, D.J., and Lawler, A. 1988. *Developmental interventions: Theories, principles, and techniques.* Columbus, Ohio: Merrill.

Durlak, J.A. 1978. Comparison between experiential and didactic methods of death education. *Omega* 9:57–66.

Feifel, H. 1977. Death and dying in modern America. *Death Education* 1:5–14.

Killilea, A.G. 1988. *The politics of human mortality.* Lexington: University of Kentucky Press.

Knott, J.E. 1979. Death education for all. In H. Wass, ed., *Dying: Facing the facts,* pp. 385–403. Washington, D.C.: Hemisphere.

LaGrand, L.E. 1988. *Changing patterns of human existence.* Springfield, Ill.: Charles C. Thomas.

Marks, S.E., and Davis, W.L. 1975. The experiential learning model and its application to large groups. In J.W. Pfeiffer and J.J. Jones, eds., *The 1975 annual handbook for group facilitators.* La Jolla, Calif.: University Associates.

Morgan, M.A. 1987. Learner-centered learning in an undergraduate interdisciplinary course about death. *Death Studies* 11:183–192.

Oshman, H.P. 1978. Death education: An evaluation of programs and techniques. *Journal supplement abstract service* (American Psychological Assocation Publication) 8:11.

Pine, V.R. 1986. The age of maturity for death education: A sociohistorical portrait of the era 1976–1985. *Death Studies* 10:209–231.

Viorst, J. 1986. *Necessary losses.* New York: Simon and Schuster.

Wass, H.; Berardo, F.M.; and Neimeyer, R.A. 1988. Dying: Integrating the facts. In H. Wass, F. Berardo, and R.A. Neimeyer, eds. *Dying: Facing the facts,* 2d ed., pp. 395–405. Washington, D.C.: Hemisphere.

Yalom, I.D. 1985. *The theory and practice of group psychotherapy.* New York: Basic Books.

1

Warm-ups and Icebreakers

IN this first chapter, a number of initial SLEs that could serve as icebreakers in a group are presented. Each can serve as a fairly uncomplicated, relatively unthreatening introduction to the general topic of death by enabling participants to engage in a brief examination of some aspect of the place of mortality in their current thought or experience. These include structured experiences with historical, developmental, or sociocultural frames of reference. Their use is most clearly recommended in early, introductory phases of a death education program or course.

1. Opening Windows

Goals

1. To enable participants to get aquainted in a nonthreatening manner.
2. To develop a climate for self-disclosure and group interaction through sharing personal information relevant to their reasons for being in a learning group dealing with death, dying, loss, or bereavement.

Setting

The group may consist of as few as eight participants to an unlimited number, with space as the factor regulating group size. The space needs to be comfortable and large enough to enable subgroups of two and four to interact without crowding or noise interference.

Time

Approximately 45 minutes.

Procedure

1. The leader discusses briefly the goals of the experience.
2. The leader instructs the group to move about the room making eye contact and interacting nonverbally but in no way talking with one another. As participants move about, they are asked to note one or two persons with whom they are not well acquainted and whom they might like to meet.
3. After about 60 seconds of milling about, the leader instructs the participants to choose a partner and signify their mutual selection nonverbally. If there is an odd number of participants, the leader can equalize by participating and pairing up with the remaining person.
4. The leader instructs the pairs to find one additional pair with whom they will form a reference group. They too should be relatively unknown to the other pair members.
5. The leader instructs the group: "With your original partner, spend the next 10 minutes describing your earliest memory of acquaintance with death—anything or anyone." After 5 minutes, the leader reminds all to be sure to allow adequate time for *both* partners to share their responses.
6. The pairs are told to switch partners with the member of the other dyad in their reference group. With that new partner, they are told: "Now I'd like you to spend the next 10 minutes discussing with your new partner some of your current beliefs about what occurs to one after death." The leader urges them to spend the bulk of their time focusing on the source or origins of influence on those beliefs.
7. Following the second dyad, the group members are told to switch partners one last time with the remaining member of the reference group. With this third partner, they share their response to the question, "When, where, how, and at what age do I expect to die?" Ten minutes is also allotted for this pairing.
8. The four members of each reference group are then instructed to regroup and to spend about 15 minutes discussing their reactions to the previous half-hour's exercise and to concentrate on their feelings about what they shared, what they learned about one another (as a person, a peer), and what they've (re-)discovered about themselves as a result.

Variations

Alternate stimulus items (such as beliefs about suicide, euthanasia, previous death losses, and so forth) could be devised. The group's composition and ultimate tasks should determine the nature of the questions used to integrate the various pairings and should build from lesser to greater risk in self-disclosure. This exercise is ideal for initial get-togethers in a course, training session, or workshop.

Debriefing

Each group is solicited (they can select a spokesperson) to comment on their observations about:

1. The difference in the conversation between early and later partners and in the full group of four on such topics as anxiety level, superficiality, contact with partner, and the nature of the disclosure that the question required.
2. What the group members learned about each other—not specific information but how they would characterize one another's needs, as well as what their observations about the experience as a whole were.

Allow the remainder of the time available for sharing these comments with the full group and for the leader to summarize and restate the purposes of the exercise so that participants can reflect on their accomplishments of those ends.

2. I'm Coming Back As . . .

Goals

1. To provide an introduction to some aspects of belief in reincarnation.
2. To introduce a new group of students to one another (icebreaker).
3. To give opportunity to the class to clarify some values of living *and* dying.

Materials

This can be conducted with or without writing responses down but seems most easily accomplished with pencil and paper for each participant.

Time

About 5 minutes per participant plus another 10–20 minutes for summary discussion.

Procedures

This SLE serves as a light way to get into the topic of death and beliefs about immortality. It can be introduced simply as a fun way to project creatively how we might "return" or "reincarnate" if we could come back after our deaths as someone or something else. It should also be stated that such fantasies often reveal some of our values and impressions of unfulfilled wishes and lifestyle variations.

Distribute paper and pencil or pen and instruct the group members thus:

I want you to let your mind, your imagination go to connect freely with some thoughts and images you've not had before. Imagine that you could have your choice of returning to "live" or "be" in this world in a new form of existence after you died.

I'm going to suggest several categories to help frame your thoughts, but other than that, you should just let yourself go to picture what reincarnated form you might wish to take. We're going to do this for about three or four different categories, and I'll give you a couple of minutes for each.

You're to state first the answer to the question and then write down under that on your paper what prompted you to select that response, what appeals about that reincarnated form.

First, if you could come back as a color, *what would that color be? Once you've chosen that color and written it down, directly under it state briefly why you made that choice. Be creative but be yourself in doing so.*

The facilitator instructs the group similarly for a couple more categories. Those that have been fruitfully used are machine, flower, bush, plant or tree, day of the week, small animal, large animal, type of automobile, historical person, and currently living person. Choose only about three or four of these as time is needed to share the answers and rationales later. It also seems helpful to proffer the categories in somewhat of a hierarchy, going from inanimate to animate things and increasing the complexity as you go.

Debriefing

Questions can be dealt with either as a whole group or in subgroups of four or more if the class is large.

1. How did you feel about this exercise?
2. Do you have strong feelings about reincarnation in some form?
3. Which of those you wrote (or some other) is fondest to you?
4. Do any of your choices reflect some unrealized wishes, some regrets or fantasies unfulfilled about your life as it has been?
5. What have you learned during this exercise about the elements of your life-style you cherish?
6. If important people in your life had the same choices, would you want them to come back as something or someone compatible or quite different? Why?
7. Have you given this or any other notion of immortality some thought before? If yes, what was the outcome?

---

3. Book Watch

Goals

To identify own and others' responses to death-titled books.

Materials

Books with death or death-related titles—usually course-related books.

Time

Single session of 30–40 minutes with 4–5 days between assignment and session.

Procedures

Assign participants-students to carry textbooks or other books that have *death* and *dying* in the title for a period of 4 to 5 days. They should take these books with them everywhere: shopping, riding the bus, meetings, and so forth. They should observe people's responses to the literature and themselves and record the verbal and nonverbal responses. The fact that there may be nonverbal responses is as important as verbal ones.

Unless absolutely necessary, the participants should not volunteer the information that the reading material is for a course in death and dying. At the conclusion of any verbal interaction, the participant should tell why he or she is carrying these books. After revealing this information, he or she should observe any change in the relationship, any tension, and so forth and note how the change occurs.

Have participants write a minimum of two pages and a maximum of six pages relating to the following information:

1. Describe the variety of responses that occurred.
2. What response was most prevalent?
3. Substantiate that the responses reflected the attitude that death is denied—or accepted—as a part of life in our society.
4. Do these general responses of others reflect your basic responses to death? If so, how? If not, why?
5. How comfortable or uncomfortable did you feel carrying out this assignment? Attempt to analyze the reason(s) for feeling the way you did.

Students can share their papers with one another.

Debriefing

1. How were your experiences similar? different? What do you see as reasons for similarities or differences?
2. In what way was the exercise useful as an introduction to this course?
3. What difficulties did you have writing your paper?
4. Would you change this exercise in any way to achieve the same results?

4. Daily Headlines

Goals

1. To expand awareness of number of everyday events associated with death and dying.
2. To increase understanding of how the media influence our attitudes about death and dying.
3. To assist in developing sensitivity and empathy for those who have experienced the death of a loved one.
4. To promote discussion about kinds of personal and social needs of individuals who have recently experienced the death of a loved one.

Every day, newspapers and other media present objective accounts of death experiences. Eventually we become desensitized to these accounts. As Stalin once observed, "A single death is a tragedy, while a million deaths is a statistic." This exercise is designed to assist participants in developing sensitivity to some of the human issues involved for those who experience the loss of a loved one.

Setting

A room large enough for participants to spread out reading materials and interact without disturbing others.

Materials

A current issue of a major daily newspaper, a pencil, and a felt-tipped pen plus a blank sheet of paper for *each* participant.

Time

Minimum 1 hour.

Procedures

1. The leader distributes a newspaper and a blank sheet of paper to each participant and tells each to scan the newspaper looking for ten different articles that describe some event that involves the death of a person. The leader instructs the participants to mark these articles with a felt-tipped pen.

2. The leader then instructs each participant to select one of the articles to examine in detail, giving the following instructions:

   The article you selected describes the objective, measurable fact of some person's death. Imagine you are able to step inside the people who are intimately involved with the story and rewrite it, describing how you believe each person might really feel about the death if each were able to verbalize it fully. First, describe how the dead person might have felt about his or her own death. Then describe how his or her loved ones might feel about the death of the person they loved. Take your time and describe as fully as you can all the feelings you think these people might experience.

3. The facilitator might allow enough time for each participant to write and describe the feelings of at least two or three people involved who are affected by the death experience. Then the participants can sit in a close circle and read aloud the original newspaper account of the death and their own written account that describes the feelings of the deceased and loved ones. They might be encouraged to read the written description slowly and with sensitivity.

Variations

Another strategy with some merit in this exercise has been suggested by Robert Kastenbaum of Arizona State University. He has students use scissors rather than markers to cut out *any* ad, article, or picture mindful of death.

Debriefing

After each participant has had an opportunity to read his or her written story, some of the following group discussion questions might be useful:

1. What was this experience like for you?
2. What was it like for you to try to imagine and describe how a dead person might have felt about his or her own death? How might loved ones feel about this death?
3. What was it like to listen to these accounts of some person's death? Did this experience stir up any feelings you might have about the deaths of people you have loved? If so, what were some of the feelings?
4. What kinds of assistance do you imagine loved ones might need to help them deal emotionally with the death of the person they loved?
5. What are some of the ways that mass media influence our attitudes and feelings about death? What kind of constructive changes might be suggested?

---

5. Death Collage

Goals

1. To have participants identify pictures and words they associate with death and life and to examine why they associate such symbols with one or the other.
2. To examine the interrelationships and/or distinctions made between life and death.

Materials

Work space, many magazines, scissors, glue, construction paper, large envelopes.

Time

Two 40-minute sessions or 1½ hours.

Procedures

Session 1

Explain to the participants that they will be making individual collages about life and death. Allow them 30–40 minutes to go through magazines and cut out as many pictures and words having to do with life and death as possible and put them in their large envelope. Participants will take envelopes with them at the end of the session. Between sessions, if this is done in two sessions, participants are encouraged to look over the pictures and words and add to them. Instruct them not to discard any items at this time.

Session 2

At the beginning of this session have participants find a work space where they can arrange items and glue them on paper to make a collage. Discards may be made at this time. No further instructions should be given. Allow 15–20 minutes for this activity. At the end of this time, assemble all participants with their collages. Have each participant explain his or her collage and answer questions.

Debriefing

1. What kinds of items did you choose to represent life? death? Were they similar or different?
2. When you looked at them between sessions, did you have any difficulty identifying which ones were death and which ones were life?
3. Did you add any words or pictures between sessions?
4. Which group of items was easier to assemble? Why?
5. Were you more aware of possible inclusions between sessions than you were before you began this exercise?
6. When you began to construct your collage, did you mix or separate life and death items?
7. Are they part of one another or separate and distinct?
8. Did you communicate with anyone about this project—either in the group or outside the group?
9. Did anyone help you or did you help anyone else? Why or why not? Who?
10. Did you have any difficulty with any part of this activity?
11. Did the choosing of pictures and words, the putting them together, and the explaining of your collage give you any perspective or insight into your own attitudes toward life and/or death?
12. Did you discard any items? If so, what items, and why? If not, why not?

---

6. Gallows Humor

Goals

1. To provide a medium for exploring societal views and treatments of death.
2. To look at some ways death is dealt with in song.
3. To initiate discussion about the taboo nature of death in some subcultures.
4. To provide some examples of death-related humor.

Early in the life of a group or class, it is often worthwhile to examine how death falls on our consciousness socially in various ways. One way of injecting some vitality into this process is by looking at how death has been portrayed in song and humor. This also enables us to look at the salutary benefits of laughing at the things that pose a threat to living.

Materials

Phonograph or tape player and recordings of the numbers cited under "Procedures."

Time   Variable; allow about 20 minutes to play a sufficient variety of themes. Then spend another 20 or so minutes debriefing.

Procedures   Introduce the topic generally, noting that we often use humor to relieve tension or to avoid anxiety-provoking thoughts and conversation with taboo areas such as sexuality and death. Emphasize that this is not altogether a bad idea. In fact, being able to see the humorous side of distasteful events has frequently been humankind's saving grace. It is an essential dimension in helping define the breadth of human nature.

Examples of humorous recordings poking fun at death's specter could include:

- Bill Cosby on "Rigor Mortis" (from his record *I Started Out as a Child*).
- "Pore Jud Is Daid" from *Oklahoma!*
- "The Funeral Tango" from *Jacques Brel Is Alive and Well.*
- Mark Twain's story "Accident Insurance" (from Hal Holbrook's album *Mark Twain Tonight*, volume 2).
- Tom Lehrer's song "We Will All Go Together When We Go" (from his album *An Evening Wasted with Tom Lehrer*).

Variations   If the group seems really interested in the possibilities of this topic, they can be divided into small groups to make group collages expressing themes like "death and humor" or "American attitudes toward death." Stacks of newspapers and magazines along with scissors, paste, poster board, and other materials can be provided. The final products can be posted and described for the whole group to engage in discussions, or an annotated list can be made and updated for sharing.

Another potent way to illustrate the integration of so-called gallows humor in the culture is through the visual medium. Many cartoonists, including those syndicated in the popular press and those found on editorial pages, offer a splendid way of introducing the viewer to humorous looks at mortality. Gary Larson, Matt Groenig, the *Ziggy* series, *Herman, Sylvia,* and many others have provided numerous cartoons that poke fun at the ironic ways humans regard death and dying. Slides could be made or collections of these cartoons could be gathered in print and shown to learners as a way of illustrating themes and provoking discussion of psychosocial responses to those issues they address. Also, these materials could be employed to trigger discussion of the role of humor in coping with life-threatening illness and loss.

Debriefing   Lyrics lend reference in different ways to cultural attitudes, postures toward death and dying, and mortality. Many harken back to a previous period; more recent tunes make contemporary statements about our collective belief system and values. Several lines of questioning can be pursued here:

1. What made the humor evident in each situation?
2. How much is fantasy a factor in these tunes?
3. What do these lyrics have to say about immortality? Aren't these recordings themselves paeans to the immortal heritage of their creators and performers?
4. What taboos are expressed in the lyrics?
5. How has cultural evolution affected our views of the sentiments expressed in these songs?
6. Did you find certain elements especially humorous? Which and why? Were others not funny to you? How?

---

7. To Die on Television

Goals

We are all exposed to multiple media deaths daily, although we are rarely involved with them personally. In many ways, this exposure may contribute to forming general attitudes toward death, but it often leaves people unprepared for the variety of feelings that accompany the personal experience of death and the mourning process. This experience attempts to make participants aware of "media death" and the attitudes and behaviors it fosters.

Materials

Paper, pencils, access to a television set, television schedule, overhead projector or chalkboard.

Time

Two sessions of 45–50 minutes each.

Procedures

Session 1

This session should include an introduction to media death and development of a schedule for viewing, as well as a check sheet or observation sheet to be used by all viewers. A schedule should be worked out to cover all channels and hours of programming, with specific groups or individuals responsible for viewing and recording observed data. After a schedule has been established, including commercials, previews, and news breaks, the group needs to determine a specific, common data collection sheet that specifies type of information to gather. This might include program identification information; actual observed deaths; type, cause, and circumstances of death; references to death; response of others; relationship of others; death vocabulary; funeral and memorial services; who is responsible for making the arrangements, if reference to them is omitted; disposal of the body; feelings described about the death or the person; social impact of the death; mourning process; whether those who died were identified by name or member of a group and identified by the group they belonged to; and whether any values were expressed about life or death.

The group may wish to focus on a single aspect or to observe a variety. Each observation should include identification information such as channel, time of day, type of program or presentation, intended audience, and length of program.

At the end of this session, each participant should have specific viewing responsibilities and a common observation sheet to be completed. Participants may decide to work in groups or alone. An attempt should be made to cover at least one consecutive 24-hour period of programming.

Session 2

The gathered data are compiled at this time using the observation sheet as a basis, with provision for recording any additional observed data. Each observation is recorded in order to gain an overall picture of media death. This should take 10–15 minutes.

After the data are compiled, the group may be subdivided into groups of three or four to examine findings and make generalizations or draw conclusions about media death. This should take 10–15 minutes. At the end of this time, each subgroup should share conclusions. The total group may wish to determine a follow-up individually or as a group.

Variation

A variation of this exercise could use the current top ten rental videos. Group members could identify the source of information, arrange for rental and viewing, construct an instrument to gather common data, and then gather and analyze data from the viewings.

Debriefing

1. Was your television viewing any different from normal? Did you notice different things?
2. Was your recreational television viewing affected by your observations?
3. Was death generally presented in a context?
4. Was it personalized?
5. What were the common causes of death?
6. In what ways were the deaths you observed similar to or different from your own experiences with death?
7. Is media death realistic? Should it be more or less realistic than it is?
8. How is death presented in children's programming? daytime shows? news? comedy? drama?
9. What life values are expressed in the reporting of deaths?
10. Do you have any specific examples of a particularly good or poor presentation of death in the media?
11. In what ways could you communicate your opinion to those responsible for programming?
12. What program suggestion would you make about the presentation of death?

8. Childhood Recollections

Goals

1. To increase awareness of how personal attitudes about death and dying develop.
2. To identify how one's present attitudes and feelings toward death and dying relate to early experience.
3. To discover the extent to which one's feelings about death and dying are shared by others.

When people discuss and explore together their personal experiences and feelings about death, they often discover that their attitudes about death and dying are shared by others. In order to explore fully one's feelings about death, a structure for exploration is often necessary.

Insofar as childhood memories are reflections of the past, exploring and discussing such memories about death and dying can be less threatening than directly discussing one's current feelings. Through the process of exploration, participants are often able to generate memories and feelings they thought they had forgotten. These early experiences can then be reviewed to determine how they might be currently influencing one's attitudes about death.

Materials

Poster paper or chalkboard on which to write discussion questions.

Time

Minimum of 1 hour.

Procedures

1. Instruct participants to form small groups of three to five members and find a comfortable location in the room.
2. Introduce the exercise:

   This activity is designed to assist us in remembering and talking about our childhood memories and experiences of death and dying. One of the purposes is to increase our awareness of how we felt about death as a child. This awareness may then help us understand our present feelings and assist us in clarifying what attitudes we might wish to change.

   You may find that you can't remember many experiences. You may also discover that someone else's memories remind you of a variety of experiences you had forgotten about.

   You may also find that there are some experiences you prefer not to discuss with your group. That is perfectly OK. Talk about only what you wish to talk about.

3. Introduce the first topic of discussion. Because some groups might require more time to discuss certain topics, allow flexibility by

writing topic headings on the chalkboard and encouraging each group to move through the topics at a pace comfortable to each. Ask them to review in their mind's eye and share as they are willing and comfortable:

What were some of your earliest experiences with death when you were a child? Was it a death of a person? a pet? What feelings do you recall about these experiences? Who did you talk to about your feelings? (pause)

How did members of your family deal with their feelings about death and dying? What particular memories do you have about how your family expressed their feelings? (pause)

What did you learn about death from your peers and close friends? (pause)

What are your memories of times when you were responsible for killing some living thing? What feelings did you have about these experiences? What feelings do you now have about these experiences? (pause)

What are your early memories of times when you thought you were going to die or be killed? What feelings did you have about these events? Who did you turn to for help?

Debriefing

The following questions can be discussed among the entire group as a way of achieving closure for the activity:

1. What have you learned about your attitudes toward death through this exercise? How do you feel about this experience?
2. What other questions might we have discussed about our childhood memories of death?
3. What might be done to assist children in exploring their attitudes and feelings about death?

9. Storytelling with Children

Goals

1. To sensitize participants to the developmental nature of the concept of death, exploring how children's reactions and understandings are different from those of adults.
2. To enable students to relate to the unique needs of children at various developmental levels.
3. To provide a supportive environment in which participants can examine their own childhood experiences with death.

Materials

Children's books and stories dealing with death and dying. A children's librarian can help to identify texts that provide background material on children's acquisition of knowledge and understanding of death.

Time	Allow sufficient time for each brief story to be presented in summary, plus at least 20 minutes for debriefing.
Procedure	Each participant should select and read a children's story with a death theme before the session. During the session, each will summarize the story and discuss the developmental level, appropriateness, theme, and whatever else seems interesting about the story. A small-group format, with six to eight members, is ideal, but this activity can be done in a large group. In the latter case, the instructor might select representative literature and assign it to a few students for reading and presentation.
Debriefing	1. Why do you think you selected the story you read? 2. Does it present death as irreversible? universal? 3. What do you remember related to death during your childhood? At what age? 4. Refer also to stories and games that illustrate a childhood belief that death is reversible and not universal ("Sleeping Beauty," "Ring around a Rosey," "Little Red Riding Hood," "Peek-a-Boo," and others). 5. How might children of different ages react to these stories? Why might there be differences by age?

10. The Funeral

Goals	To observe, attend, and reflect upon institutionalized practices related to funeral services.
Materials	A recent local newspaper.
Time	1 week between assignment and group session.
Procedure	Have participants read the obituaries in the newspaper and select the funeral of a stranger to be held at a church, mortuary, synagogue, or temple at a time convenient for them to attend. Suggest they attend a service that provides an opportunity to observe institutionalized practices with which they are not highly familiar, such as those of another faith. After they attend the funeral, the participants should write a brief report of their observations and personal reactions to the service. At the beginning of the next session, they share the reports.

Special Instructions

1. Before attending the funeral or immediately after, participants who are unfamiliar with the religious affiliation of the person whose

funeral they attended should find information about the religious practices related to death.

2. The obituary notice should be provided with each report.
3. *No more than* two participants should go to any one funeral.
4. If two participants attend a funeral together, each should submit a separate paper. They should not consult each other.
5. Each report should identify the following:

   ■ The social purposes of the funeral that were evident in this particular service. Give examples of each purpose cited.
   ■ The particular religious, social, and cultural rituals for assisting grieving in the funeral service.
   ■ How the funeral seemed to assist the bereaved with the grieving process, and how it seemed to interfere.
   ■ The social values in evidence at this funeral.
   ■ The behavioral responses toward death and/or grieving of those attending and officiating at the funeral. Upon what attitudes might these behavioral responses be based?
   ■ Your own reactions to and feelings at the funeral. Attempt to relate your understanding of the basis for these feelings and reactions.

Debriefing

1. What was this experience as a whole like for you?
2. What did you hear that was new to your experiences of institutionalized practices related to death? What was familiar?
3. Was any aspect especially appealing or unappealing to you?
4. In what ways are institutionalized practices particularly responsive or unresponsive to human or social needs?
5. What changes would you make in institutionalized practices? Why?

---

11. Journal

Goals

1. To provide an opportunity for ongoing personal reflection and writing.
2. To identify patterns, puzzles, questions, answers, ideas, feelings, and resources.
3. To record and perhaps share growth, change, self-knowledge, new learning, and old learnings newly rediscovered.
4. To provide the facilitator with a regular, informal, nonthreatening means of communication and feedback from and with individuals in an ongoing group.

Materials

A notebook, diary, or other book with blank pages for each person.

Time

At least 30 minutes between sessions. Could be short daily entries or one or more longer entries weekly.

Procedures   Participants record reflections about each session between sessions. These journals should have no format requirements and should allow participants to write freely about the group experience, as well as any feelings, insights, observations, questions, answers, new learnings, new insights into old learnings, and any other related topic.

Journals should be read regularly by the facilitator with any needed follow-up noted. It is often helpful for the facilitator to write answers, comments, and reflections to each writer. The journals should remain a confidential and individual form of communication between participant and facilitator.

Variations   Journal entries can be shared with other group members at the beginning of each session on a voluntary basis *or* group members can form dyads and share journals with one another at some point in each session.

Audio cassettes can offer a quick, vocal form of exchange, including commentary with corresponding peers or group leaders; however, it can also be a more cumbersome way to document a longitudinal set of entries of great number or length. Obviously, this format requires audiotapes and recorders.

Debriefing   This can take place regularly through reading, writing, and comments. At the end of the group sessions, the following questions would be a useful form of debriefing:

1. Was the journal helpful?
2. Was it easy or difficult? How?
3. What would you change or do differently?
4. Were comments helpful, or would you prefer no comments?
5. What types of entries did you make most often?
6. Did you share anything in your journal with others in the group? outside the group? If so, what prompted this sharing? What was the response? Would you share it again?
7. Will you continue to keep a journal? Why or why not?

---

12. Mything Death

Goals   1. To have participants write and illustrate death myths and construct a book containing all of the participants' stories.
2. To examine existing and original death myths.

Materials   Paper, construction or drawing paper, pens or pencils, typewriter, crayons, markers, cardboard, magazines, tables, scissors, glue, copier, clasp folders, hole punch.

Time	Two 40-minute sessions.

Procedures

Session 1

This exercise is designed to accompany a mythology lesson. After a study of the origin, purpose, and use of myths and some specific myths, participants, either alone or in groups of not more than three, will write a myth that explains some aspect of death. This work may take a full 40-minute session. If some participants finish before the time, have them title, type, and illustrate their myth. Encourage original drawings, but allow the use of pictures cut from magazines.

Session 2

Each participant should come to this session with a titled, typed, and illustrated myth. Myths are read aloud and questions are answered by the author(s). The entire group then decides upon an order for their mythology book. All myths should be included.

One of two things can happen at this point: (1) a single book can be constructed with small groups being responsible for various sections (cover design and construction, contents, author information, foreword, glossary, index, introduction, dedication, pagination and sequencing); or (2) if a copier is available, copies of all myths can be made for each student. While copies are being made, each participant will design his or her own cover, contents, dedication, author information, and so on. When copies are made, each participant will put together his or her own book. Participants may then share those individually designed parts of their books.

Variation

Participants may wish to find and use existing myths and/or mythological figures that symbolically represent or interpret death in different cultures and during different times.

Debriefing

1. Was it hard to think of a myth to explain death?
2. What symbols or symbolic persons did you choose for your myth? Why?
3. Why did you illustrate your myth in this particular way? Is there anything in your personal experience that helped you when you wrote?
4. What were the advantages and disadvantages of working in a group or alone?
5. How did you react when you heard and saw the other myths?
6. Why did you think the myths in this book were ordered in the way they were?
7. Why did you choose the dedication you did for this book?
8. Was it more difficult or easier to write the other parts of the book?
9. What attitude toward death is expressed in this book?

10. Is the book in general similar to or different from your attitude toward death?
11. To what audience would this book appeal? Describe by age, sex, background, and other characteristics.
12. Can you think of a person you know to whom you might lend or give this book? Why?
13. Is the myth you wrote consistent with your view of death? Why/why not?

Note: This can be used in conjunction with the study of mythology, history, creative writing, language study, art, anthropology, psychology, or social studies.

---

13. Ethnographic Interviews

Goals

To examine various customs related to death, funerals, and burial and explore the cultural attitudes and attendant rituals through interviews with a variety of people.

Materials

Paper, pens or pencils, markers, large sheets of newsprint, tape.

Time

Three 40-minute sessions.

Procedure

Session 1

Have participants break into groups of four or five. Groups should decide what aspects of death, funeral, and burial they will investigate as a group, where they will locate the population to be interviewed, and the number of interviews to be conducted. Each member should do at least five interviews. Individuals could be interviewed as well as representatives of death-related businesses (florists, funeral directors, clergy, cemetery personnel, obituary writers, musicians, printers, casket makers). The group should determine the interview format, questions, and individual responsibilities of group members. If group members have never done interviews before, this would be a good time to give interview guidelines and practice with one another.

Session 2

This session should take place at least a week after the first session to allow enough time for all interviews to be completed. During this session, group members should compile interview findings and make generalizations or draw conclusions from their findings. They should also prepare visual materials or handouts for presentation to the whole group at the third session.

Session 3
At this time each group will present its findings and explain its interview process, population, and how it arrived at its conclusions or generalizations. The total group will then compare findings and identify areas of support or conflict and attempt to make some general observations about death, funeral, and burial rituals based on interview findings. Group members may wish to share any interesting individual encounters while interviewing. Discussion should follow.

Variations

1. In groups of four to six participants construct a questionnaire on death to use to interview students, teachers, parents, and members of the community. The questionnaire should attempt to find out how society has an impact on values and attitudes toward death. Each group should contact at least twenty people, or five interviews per participant. Allow 1 week for construction of the questionnaire, interviews, and tallying of results.

   The questions can serve as a guide for inquiry into society's view toward death and life. After sharing results, participants write their own perspective toward death and share this with others. Discussion follows.

2. Each participant interviews three to four people about their personal experiences with a death in their family. The participants should attempt to interview people of different age, sex, occupation, marital status, religion, and ethnic backgrounds. In talking with these individuals, participants should try to learn the following: (1) How has the individual experienced death in his or her family (how many, who, when, where, what circumstances, type of death). (2) Was any one death in the family especially significant to the individual? (3) What were the initial and prolonged reactions of the individual and of the family to the death? What initial and long-range effect did the death have on the individual? on the family? (4) Did the individual and the family go through a period of mourning? Were there any special rituals or activities following the death?

   Following the interviews, either in a paper or discussion, participants should: (1) define crises and identify whether the death identified by the individual was a crisis for the individual and/or the family; (2) compare and contrast the grief and mourning responses of the interviewees. Using theory from readings on grief reaction to establish criteria for normal and abnormal grief, identify if these responses were normal or abnormal grief reactions. Substantiate the type of grief with data from the interviews; (3) discuss reactions and difficulties encountered in talking with individuals interviewed. If no difficulties were encountered, discuss why there were none.

3. Identify several local ethnic or cultural groups. Arrange to interview representatives or spokespersons for these groups in order to

identify and explore differences in attitudes and practices related to death and dying.

Debriefing

1. How did you determine who you would interview?
2. What did you want to find out in your interviews?
3. Why did you think that your specific population would help you find this out?
4. How did you decide what questions to ask?
5. What happened when you approached people? What was their response to the topic? to you? How would you have responded to such an approach?
6. What did you find to be unique about the population you interviewed?
7. Were your results what you thought they would be?
8. Were there areas of agreement? conflict?
9. Was there any note of difference between past and current practices?
10. How did you feel asking questions about death?
11. Did you find out anything about your own practices in relation to the population interviewed?
12. What influence does society or family have on attitudes and practices at time of death?

2 Instrumental Exercises and Applied Designs

THIS chapter contains forms and applied designs that require some writing on the part of participants. Their focus is a written reflection on some aspect of life-style or death-style. By reflecting on different temporal perspectives, the learner can resynthesize personal data through analyzing both past events and future possibilities having to do with dying, death, or other loss experiences. They represent a range of effective demands but are clearly a notch above the initial exercises in their call on learners' energies. Thus, they should be attempted only where there is both shared knowledge and trust that has come from a group having had some time to experience together. A thorough summary activity is critical.

1. Life Lines: The View from Now

Goals

1. To enable participants to obtain graphic perspectives on their development to date and future aspirations.
2. To provide a pointed chronicle of the impacts of signal events: birth, deaths, losses, gains in people's lives.
3. To afford an opportunity to plan one's "remaining" time as a new, and perhaps revised, future prospect in the face of past events.

Materials

Pencil, pen or, if possible, two or three differently colored markers for each participant; "Life Lines" form or model on a board or on a flip-chart the general arrangement of lines and polar labels.

Time

Variable, but 20–30 minutes minimum is needed by each person to complete a chart, and another 30 minutes to debrief the experience, first in small groups and then in summary with all.

Procedures

Share the goals of this exercise and then have participants proceed on their own before convening subgroups. Instruct them as follows:

> *Using the printed form, first label the key events of your life from birth to this day on top of the first line, while marking the year (and month, if possible) of each just below it. Space them according to some appropriate proportion, or distance both in relation to one another temporally and with overall respect to the total time the line encompasses. These events are those* you *view as signal or pivotal, important happenings in your past, which had a strong meaning for or impact on you.* [If using multiple colors, encourage different ones to be used for date and event. Pause about 15 minutes and then give the next instructions. Or these can be given as a continuing part of the preliminary directions.]
>
> *Once you've filled and labeled the top line to your satisfaction, go to the bottom line. Starting at the extreme right end, date your plausible year of death. Then go to the left-hand end and insert today's date. Proceed in a similar way to label and date your projected future, attending to such fantasies with reasonable spacing. Pay attention, too, to the expected loss events involving marriages of children, deaths of others of importance, and life-style changes wished for in that possible future.*

An option here, as they complete the second line, is to ask them to go back over each line and circle the one or two most profound experiences of the past and the one or two most wanted aspirations of the future. When this is done, a later question for discussion can center on each person's criteria for selection.

For those who object to the linearity and unidirectionality of a pair of lines, an alternative basic figure can be used. One that offers such a variation is a helical, spiral, or coil figure. It can be placed on either the vertical or horizontal, with dates and labels on opposite sides of the coil. Or the date can be placed inside the spiral, and events appraised (retrospectively) as negative placed on one side of the spiral, with positive ones on the other (top versus bottom or right versus left sides, respectively). This may resolve the linearity problem and also provide different visual imagery more in keeping with some people's notions of an event's felt impact.

Debriefing

Usually in pairs or groups of three or four (maximum), the exercise can be debriefed with the following kinds of inquiry directed by the facilitator:

1. How difficult or easy was this exercise?
2. Was the experience:

   - Enjoyable or painful?
   - Enlightening or affirming?
   - Something you think of often?

3. What mode of death or dying did you choose for yourself? Why?
4. What prompted your selection of the time for your death?
5. What patterns emerged in reviewing the past (losses, gains, maturational transformations, etc.)?
6. Did your learn anything about yourself or your life-style as a result of completing this SLE?
7. If you had it to redo, what would change? In what ways do you see your projected future as compensating for deficits felt in the past?

Life Lines: The View from Now

Birth
Date

Today's
Date

Today's
Date

Death
Date

---

2. Coping with Personal Loss

Goals

1. To examine the loss experience of participants.
2. To explore the emotional sequelae to reconciled as well as unresolved losses.
3. To discover the aspects of "surviving" significant losses that lead to growth—the "loss-to-gain" phenomenon.
4. To share the means and methods used to cope with varying losses.

Setting

Circular seating for subgroups of no more than six or seven.

Materials

A copy of the activity worksheet, "Coping with Personal Loss: Self-Inventory," for each participant, plus a pen or pencil for each.

Time

1 hour or about 10 minutes for each member of the group. (Note group size limitations recommended.)

Procedures

Introduce the SLE as "an opportunity to examine retrospectively the various loss histories people have experienced." Then distribute the self-inventory and a writing instrument (as needed) to each participant. If the group is larger than six or so, subgroups of no fewer than four should be arranged. Thus, when the group size exceeds eight, such arrangements are desirable, with the instructions, and later questions in the debriefing phase, led by a single facilitator.

The discussion of the written responses can take either of two basic formats:

1. With a discussion of each participant's complete responses going on in turn, or, preferably perhaps, a comparable response can be sought from each group member for each of the three losses listed.
2. The use of the A, B, and C sections in a manner of orchestrating the loss-to-gain "lessons" for each person.

Whatever approach is used, illumination of the goals for this exercise with optimal representation of each group member and with a maximization of the variety of losses and responses to them is the desirable outcome.

Debriefing

1. Did you notice that the nature of the lost object only partially dictates intensity and complexity of the emotional experience that follows? Cite examples.
2. To what extent was the age at loss a critical developmental factor in the loss experience?
3. What were the forms of coping used? How successful with what losses was each of these?
4. How critical has the passage of time proved to be in the loss-resolution experience?
5. What experiential lessons can be compared to grief and bereavement theory from this set of discussions?

Coping with Personal Loss: Self-Inventory

A. List three significant losses you have personally sustained in your life thus far. Don't consider just people; also think about the loss of tangible objects, as well as intangibles such as certain hopes, aspirations, beliefs, attitudes, and the like. Note your age at the time of the loss (in parentheses at the end):

1. _____ (   )

2. _____ (   )

3. _____ (   )

B. Decide where you are intellectually and emotionally with respect to each of those three losses, and mark an "X" on the corresponding line below to designate to what degree each is still having a regular impact on your living as you note its lingering effects (if any). Then write a word or two on that line to label the feeling describing your overall sense of that effect.

No noticeable effect   Major noticeable effect

1. _____

2. _____

3. _____

C. Describe below briefly and concisely how any one (you choose) of the losses above has been dealt with in the course of your grieving. Have you "gained" anything as a result? In what ways specifically? Any surprises?

_____

_____

_____

_____

_____

_____

_____

_____

3. Death and Dying: A Brief Personal Inventory

Goals
1. To provide some data for further examination about some of an individual's perceptions and experiences about dying and death.
2. To identify personal issues and topical interests in this subject matter.
3. To offer a rough gauge for comparing preliminary data and later responses to some central topics and viewpoints.

Materials
Copy of the worksheet, "A Brief Personal Inventory," plus pencil or pen for each participant.

Time
Usually 10–20 minutes to complete individually.

Procedures
Aside from an introduction to the exercise, this inventory can be used to:

- Gather data solely for the facilitator to acquire a knowledge of the range of experiences, beliefs, and questions of the participants at an early point in the class or program.
- Give the instrument for completion at the beginning and again at the conclusion of a course or workshop and to note changes. This presumes a sufficient passage of time for such comparisons to be drawn validly.

The participants can share their responses with one another, in small groups or with the total group.

Debriefing
The facilitator who chooses to share the group's answers may use pairs or small groups of four to six maximum, to do some charting of the group's range of responses, particularly on numerically based questions, or even remark on change units where a preformat or postformat is employed.

Questions useful in milking this experience for more than the written responses might center on such issues as sources of influence on certain items (parental, cultural, age, religion, etc.). If field trips to funeral services, mortuaries, cemeteries, and so forth are employed as part of the course or workshop, those impacts on certain items can be discussed and elaborated at some length. Also propose assigning subsequent in-depth studies or papers or team presentations on topics or attitudes of common interest or opposite positions.

A Brief Personal Inventory

1. At what age do you consider death no longer premature? Why?

   _____

   _____

   _____

   _____

2. Are your parents still living? If no to either, please list who has died, when, at what age (yours and theirs at time of death), and the cause of death.

   _____

   _____

   _____

   _____

3. What life-threatening or life-endangering behaviors do you engage in?

   _____

   _____

   _____

   _____

4. Cite any bioethical quandaries (such as suicide, euthanasia, abortion) that you are personally concerned about, and briefly state why it is a concern.

   _____

   _____

   _____

5. Have you made a will yet? If yes, what is your relationship to the primary beneficiary?

   _____

6. Who died in your most recent death experience? When and under what circumstances did death occur?

   _____

7. At what age and in what year do you anticipate your death might occur?

   Age: _____   Year: _____

A Brief Personal Inventory (Continued)

---

8. If you could choose it, *where* and *how* would you prefer your death occur?

_____

_____

9. What is your preferred mode of body disposition at death (burial, cremation, other)?

_____

10. My expectations for afterlife are:

_____

_____

11. My questions and concerns about death, dying, bereavement, or grief are:

_____

_____

_____

_____

_____

_____

---

4. Longevity Calculation

Goals

1. To assist participants in looking at life expectancy, interpersonal differences, and influencing factors.
2. To assist learners in identifying personal life-style choices and hereditary influences on longevity.
3. To stimulate discussion of variations in personal morbidity and mortality experience.

Most of us have become aware of the demonstrated links between life-style and the likelihood of premature death. Nonetheless, most of us also still presume that personal death lies many years away, and we all hope or expect long lives. This SLE provides a method for examining some issues and quantitative data for projecting one's life expectancy. This simple exercise can provoke much personal thought and will enable discussion of the relationship between how we live and how long we might live.

Materials

Blank paper or the items listed under "Procedures" on a prepared form, plus a pen or pencil for each participant.

Time

45 minutes.

Debriefing

This can be accomplished in small groups if the total number is ten or more.

1. What was it like to be computing how long *you* might expect to live?
2. How does the age you arrived at through the exercise compare to that you imagined at the outset? What might account for differences?
3. Which of the life expectancy criteria had special relevance for you and your final projected age?
4. If you were to make any adjustments now in your style of living, what would they be, and why?

Procedures
---

1. Introduce this exercise by restating the goals listed above and then asking participants to estimate at what age they expect to die. Have them write that figure down.
2. Then instruct the participants to go through the following procedure to predict systematically their possible life expectancy. Mention that this is a set of items with weights like those used in other health risk assessments, but less scientific than some others in its calculations. In other words, it is to be regarded as impressionistic, not precise. If a particular item does not describe them or call for a mathematical change, they should go on to the next one.
   1. Start with 75; write it down.
   2. If you're female, add 4; if male, subtract 3.
   3. If you're over 35 now, add 1; if over 65, add 3.
   4. If you're nonwhite, subtract 1.
   5. If any grandparent lived to 85, add 2. If all four lived to at least 80, add 4.
   6. If either parent died of stroke or heart attack before 60, subtract 3.
   7. If any parent or sibling has/had cancer or a heart ailment, subtract 2. If any has/had diabetes, subtract 2.
   8. If you are over 60 and active or working at something you enjoy, add 2.
   9. If you completed college, add 1; if you completed a graduate degree, add 2.
   10. If you live in an urban area, subtract 2; in a town of fewer than 30,000 people, add 1.
   11. If you work at a sedentary job, subtract 2.
   12. If you get moderately vigorous exercise for 20–30 minutes at least 3 times per week, add 3.
   13. If you are married, add 2. If female, subtract 1 for every 5 years you've lived alone from ages 23–53. If male, subtract 2 for each 5 years alone from 23–53.
   14. If you sleep 6–8 hours most nights, add 2. If you routinely get fewer than 6 or more than 8 hours of sleep, subtract 3.
   15. Are you basically satisfied with life? Add 2; if not, subtract 2.
   16. Are you easily angered, and explosively responsive? If so, subtract 3; if not, add 2.
   17. Have you had a speeding ticket in the past year? Subtract 1 if yes. Add 1 if you always wear seatbelts; subtract 1 if you don't.
   18. Do you drink more than two alcoholic beverages a day or more than fourteen in a week? Subtract 3.
   19. Do you smoke more than ten cigarettes a day? Subtract 3; more than 20, subtract 5. Quit over 2 years ago? Add 2. Never smoked? Add 3.

20. Overweight by 50 pounds? Subtract 4; by 30 or more pounds, subtract 3, and by 15–29 pounds, subtract 2. If you have a low-fat, high-fiber diet, add 3. If high fat, low fiber, or both, subtract 3.
21. Women: If you have a pap smear at least every 2 years, add 2; do monthly breast self-exam, add 2. Men: Add 1 each if you do regular testicular self-exam and after 40 have annual rectal exams.
22. Use mood-lifting medications regularly? Subtract 2.
23. If you know your blood pressure, add 1. If it is within normal limits, add 1 more.
24. If you know your cholesterol, add 1. If it is under 200, add 1 more.
25. If you are a loner, lacking at least two close friends, subtract 2.
26. Subtract 1 *each* if you own a gun or engage in a risky activity like sky or scuba diving, hitchhiking, motorcycle riding, or racing motor vehicles.

3. If participants have kept a running tally, they should now have a calculated life expectancy figure. Instruct them to go back over the items and circle any they lost points for. This should help highlight areas they could scrutinize for possible life-style choice changes that could improve both the quality and quantity of their life.
4. With a mixed sex group, it is often illustrative of traditional sex differences to make a pair of lists for all to see that shows all the calculated ages as participants call them out. A member of each sex can also be asked to calculate the average of the opposite sex subgroup simultaneously.

5. Certifying Life

Goals

1. To provide a projective experience that enables people to reflect on their versions of personally appropriate or probable death-styles.
2. To expose individuals to a pertinent medicolegal document—its purpose and content—as an educational consideration.

Materials

A copy of the local form certifying death and a pencil or pen for each participant. (A typical certificate of death is reproduced here and can be used.)

Time

Approximately 30 minutes to instruct and complete and another 45 minutes to debrief.

Procedures

This is a commonly used tool for enabling people to clarify their attitudes and to envision some scenarios for their deaths and "dying trajectories."

There are several ways to use the instrument. Briefly, the certificate can be introduced as a "a once-in-a-lifetime experience. The next time your name appears on this kind of document, you'll not be able to read or contemplate it. You'll be dead. And your freedom of choice for the exercise here won't exist then!"

Following that introduction, the facilitator shares the goals of the SLE and distributes the forms. Then he or she quickly touches on each of the lines and categories to be completed, explaining each where the meaning is not clear. Each participant is to complete the death certificate, after which discussion and sharing of responses proceeds.

Variations

Participants might be given the assignment of locating a blank death certificate form from a medical facility, a state office, a local agency, a funeral director, a hospice, or a consumer group. Debriefing would then begin with identifying the source of each participant's form and by examining the process each participant went through to obtain it. Reactions and difficulties encountered in this process are part of the debriefing.

This exercise can be given as a homework assignment and then debriefed in the next meeting. Or it can be varied by asking each participant to think first of a living loved one and then to fill out the form for that person as they think or hope death might occur. Or they can fill it out either as "expected" or "hoped for" either using self or a significant other as decedent.

The latter variations pose some difficulty at times. Children particularly are resistant due to some "magical thinking" fears and superstitions. Also, at times some participants balk at their own certificate, as that too engenders some fearful concerns. The facilitator must be

Certificate of Death

	LOCAL FILE NUMBER				STATE FILE NUMBER	

DECEDENT

DECEASED — FIRST NAME	MIDDLE	LAST	SEX	DATE OF DEATH (Month, day, year)
1			2	3

7a _____

RACE — White, Black, American Indian, Etc. (Specify)	AGE — LAST BIRTHDAY (Years)	UNDER 1 YEAR		UNDER 1 DAY		DATE OF BIRTH (Month, day, year)	CITY, TOWN, OR LOCATION OF DEATH
		MOS	DAYS	HOURS	MIN		
4	5a	5b		5c		6	7a

7b _____

HOSPITAL OR OTHER INSTITUTION NAME (If not in either, give street and number)	WAS DECEDENT EVER IN U.S. ARMED FORCES? (Specify Yes or No) NAME WAR
7b	8

14 _____

CITY, TOWN STATE, OF BIRTH (If not in U.S.A. name country)	CITIZEN OF WHAT COUNTRY	MARRIED, NEVER MARRIED, WIDOWED, DIVORCED (Specify)	SPOUSE (if wife, give maiden name)
9a	9b	10	11

CT _____

SOCIAL SECURITY NUMBER	USUAL OCCUPATION (Give kind of work done during most of working life, even if retired)	KIND OF BUSINESS OR INDUSTRY
12	13a	13b

MAILING ADDRESS OF RESIDENCE — STREET OR R.F.D. AND NUMBER, CITY OR TOWN, STATE, ZIP CODE	CITY OR TOWN OF RESIDENCE (if different from mailing address)
14a	14b

PARENTS

FATHER — FIRST NAME	MIDDLE	LAST	MOTHER — FIRST NAME	MIDDLE	MAIDEN NAME
15			16		

INFORMANT — NAME	MAILING ADDRESS (Street or R.F.D No., city or town, state, zip)
17a	17b

DISPOSITION

BURIAL, CREMATION, REMOVAL, OTHER (Specify)	CEMETERY OR CREMATORY — NAME AND LOCATION	CITY OR TOWN STATE
18a	18b	

FUNERAL DIRECTOR — LICENSEE (Signature)	FUNERAL HOME — NAME AND ADDRESS (Street or R.F.D. no. city or town, state, zip)
19a	19b

CERTIFIER

To be Completed by CERTIFYING PHYSICIAN Only

To the best of my knowledge, death occurred at the time, date and place and due to the cause(s) stated	DEGREE OR TITLE	DATE SIGNED (Month, day, year)	HOUR OF DEATH
20a (Signature)		20b	20c M
NAME AND ADDRESS OF CERTIFIER (Type or print)		WAS DEATH REFERRED TO MEDICAL EXAMINER (Specify Yes or No)	IF HOSP. OR INST. Indicate DOA, OP/Emer. Rm., Inpatient (Specify)
20d		21a	21b
NAME AND ADDRESS OF ATTENDING PHYSICIAN IF OTHER THAN CERTIFIER (Type or Print)			LENGTH OF ATTENDANCE (Specify) (Hrs., wks., mo., yrs.)
22			23

REGISTRAR

REGISTRAR	DATE RECEIVED BY REGISTRAR (Mo., day, yr.)
24a (Signature)	24b

CAUSE OF DEATH

25 IMMEDIATE CAUSE (ENTER ONLY ONE CAUSE PER LINE FOR (a), (b), AND (c).)	Interval between onset and death

PART I

(a)	
DUE TO, OR AS A CONSEQUENCE OF: (Intermediate cause)	Interval between onset and death
(b)	
DUE TO, OR AS A CONSEQUENCE OF: (Underlying cause)	Interval between onset and death
(c)	

OTHER SIGNIFICANT CONDITIONS — Conditions contributing to death but not related to cause given in PART I (a)	AUTOPSY (Yes or No)	If yes were findings considered in determining cause of death
PART II	26a	26b

ACCIDENT (Specify Yes or No)	DATE OF INJURY (Mo.,day, yr.)	HOUR OF INJURY	DESCRIBE HOW INJURY OCCURRED
27a	27b	27c M	27d
INJURY AT WORK (Specify Yes or No)	PLACE OF INJURY — At home, farm, street, factory, office building, etc. (Specify)	LOCATION STREET OR R.F.D NO CITY OR TOWN STATE	
27e	27f	27g	

BRIEF INSTRUCTIONS ON REVERSE SIDE

Law requires Funeral Director to file this certificate with the City or Town Clerk at the Place of Death within 7 days

---

				PERMIT NUMBER

BURIAL-TRANSIT PERMIT   DEPARTMENT OF HEALTH

PERMIT MUST Accompany Remains to DESTINATION

DECEASED — Name FIRST	MIDDLE	LAST	SEX	DATE OF DEATH (Month, day, year)

RACE	AGE	PLACE OF DEATH (City or town, state)	

BURIAL, CREMATION, REMOVAL, OTHER (Specify)	CEMETERY OR CREMATORY — NAME AND LOCATION	CITY OR TOWN STATE

FUNERAL DIRECTOR — LICENSEE (Signature)	FUNERAL HOME — Name and Address (Street or R.F.D no., city or town, state, zip)

SEXTON must return permit to City or Town Clerk at Place of Disposal on Fifth of Next Month

CERTIFICATION: I certify that death occurred from Natural causes (see over), that referral to the Medical Examiner is not required, and that permission is hereby granted to dispose of this body

Signature of certifying Physician	Degree or title	Date signed

Authorized disposition as stated above occurred on (Date)	Tomb	Lot	Signature of Sexton or Person in Charge of Cemetery

THIS PERMIT VALID ONLY IF SIGNED BOTH BY PHYSICIAN AND BY FUNERAL DIRECTOR

aware of such responses and must allow for wide latitude and even nonresponding behavior from some.

Debriefing

This SLE seems best approached first as a personal statement of life-style and legacy. Then discussion and sharing of responses can be more readily undertaken.

On life-style, the following question may be useful to ponder: "What does your choice of time [age] and mode of death say to you about your ways of living, your way of dying, and your implicit plans for future [or the *other* if not a personal certificate]?"

---

6. Tombstone Epitaph

Goals

To enable each participant to make a personal statement that reflects life goals, personal values, and vision of immortality.

Materials

For each participant, a sheet of paper roughly 8½ × 11 inches with a facsimile of the illustration shown here and a pen, pencil, or marker.

Time

45 minutes.

Procedures

Give each participant a copy of the tombstone worksheet. Emphasize that "brevity is the soul of wit." Challenge each participant to capture their epitaph in simple, clever, and straightforward words, using any form of narrative or verse that would fit, both literally and symbolically.

Debriefing

Because this is basically an exercise involving projection—into the future as well as the past—processing of this SLE is best accomplished in ways that maximize the interpretation and understanding of what is being said on each tombstone. The group can display all their epitaphs for perusal by the total group, sharing explanations of them one at a time after all tour the "gallery." Or groups of participants up to about eight people (maximum) can alternately elaborate on the meanings and rationale behind their words. Questions might focus on the three major goals for this experience: how the epitaph represents each person's views of their social and personal values, their future life objectives as currently viewed, and their outlook on personal and specie immortality.

Worksheet

On the tombstone above, write your name and the epitaph you would like to have written on your monument. In other words, write what you would like to be remembered for.

7. The Consequences of My Dying

Goals
1. To help learners clarify their values as they contemplate the psychosocial consequences of their own deaths.
2. To enable participants to examine cultural influences on their beliefs about the impacts of death.
3. To gather some information about the relative importance of personal versus familial and social aspects of individual and group attitudes toward mortality.

Materials

A chalkboard, newsprint, or blank transparency and projector, plus paper and pen or pencil for each participant; or the worksheet "Possible Consequences of One's Own Death" can be copied for distribution to each participant.

Time

50–60 minutes.

Procedures
1. Give some history to the worksheet items and the general thrust of research in this area of thanatology. This introduction should cite the 1961 study by James Diggory and Doreen Rothman ("Values Destroyed by Death," *Journal of Abnormal Psychology* 63: 205–210), a classic piece of early research into differences of adults' views of the consequences of personal dying. More than twenty-five years have passed since this study, but the context and the questions posed are timelessly salient. The researchers asked respondents to rank the relative importance of seven statements about their own dying as personally felt values. This session will not be quite the same, but the issues themselves are quite relevant. Other researchers have investigated a myriad of themes focused on similar questions of attitude toward dying, death, grief, and afterlife, with widely varying findings, even in the same or similar cultures.
2. Show the seven items (or distribute the worksheet) and instruct participants thus:

    You are to read the seven statements about the possible consequences of your dying, and, on the scale below it, list the corresponding letter above the place that states your perception of each one's relative importance to you now. For example, you might list letter A above "1" to signify it was the statement that held the least importance or value for you among the seven, and so on down the line. Once you have done so, wait for the rest of the group to complete theirs before proceeding.

3. When all have finished, the leader, using a similar blank scale, can construct a group ranking by soliciting the numbers of people who

had each letter ranked at each position. This can also be done by making a grid of items by numbers selecting first, second, and so on. In this way, weights can be used to calculate the overall sentiments of the group. Remember if you use the scale that the largest numbers correspond to the most-valued items, while the grid method yields higher scores for least-valued statements.

4. Divide into subgroups of three or four sharing personal responses to each item, one at a time, and then discussing their reactions to differences in valuing, as well as their views of the overall group profile(s) as scaled by the leader.

5. The leader can recalculate for different profiles scaled by marital and/or family status, by sex differences or by age. These often prove illustrative of the differences influenced by sociodemographic variants.

6. Finally, after about a 20-minute small group discussion, the groups are instructed to turn to debriefing the activity. Summary reactions should be solicited from different people and groups at the conclusion. This last phase of debriefing and summary takes about 15 more minutes.

   In looking at the seven items after they are ranked and tallied, it is sometimes useful for the leader to paraphrase them for the purpose of giving participants an alternative way of conceptualizing the meanings of the statements. Thus, statement *A* can be labeled or considered "extinction of me," or "the death of all experience" for me. *B* can be called the "unknown in the afterlife." *C* is the "physical aftermath of death on my body, or maybe for some, merely "body disposition." *D* is "responsibility for others' care," or "my dependence needs." *E* is "their pain at my loss" or "grief for others." *F* is "the death of my future" or the "death of my plans." or perhaps the "threat to my legacy," while *G* is "my pain" or "painful dying." For some, these variants speak more meaningfully than the original statements.

Debriefing

1. As most groups, including the original sample studied, usually assign more value to the effects on others, examine how you ranked those items as opposed to the individual impact items. What accounts for the differences?

2. What do you (and most other people, in your estimation) want to be your legacies (in a nontangible sense) to others?

3. Is there a perceived irony in the relative positions or importance of items *F* and *A*? Aren't they coterminous?

4. If you looked at differences by age, sex, marital, or family status, what accounts for those in each case? Did or will you feel differently at another time? How and why?

5. What possible changes in your behavior or beliefs may result from this experience?

Possible Consequences of One's Own Death

A. I could no longer have any experiences.
B. I am uncertain what might happen to me if there is a life after death.
C. I am afraid of what might happen to my body after death.
D. I could no longer care for my dependents or loved ones.
E. My death would cause grief to my relatives and friends.
F. All my plans and projects would come to an end.
G. The process of dying might be painful.

SCALE

1	2	3	4	5	6	7
(Least important)					(Most important)	

---

3 Values Clarification and Affective Experiences

This chapter offers a range of introspective and variously intense experiences. All require at least a moderate amount of participant self-disclosure, and they focus on the many nuances of living in the shadow of death and dying.

A thorough consideration of the group's readiness for delving into such material is warranted. Facilitators are urged to use these SLEs only after some period of initial acquaintance and interaction has been accomplished. Some of these are similar in a few respects to role-playing exercises, although the "roles" to be assumed are personal and not to be acted.

1. Dying Times

Goals

1. To examine two sets of sociodemographic data pertinent to the study of death differences by sex and over time.
2. To generate discussion of reasons for historical differences in human mortality by age and sex in the United States.

Materials

The two data sets for this activity can be used as print copies or reproduced as slides or transparencies.

Time

45 minutes or less.

Procedures

1. Give the tables to the participants, and instruct them to write down individually *three things for each table* that seem remarkable to them as they ponder the data's meanings (15–20 minutes).

2. Divide into subgroups of four or five to share observations (10–15 minutes). They need not reach consensus but should be prepared to offer some shared group comments when the full group reconvenes. Perhaps a spokesperson should be selected early in the discussion.

Debriefing

1. What specific factors have led to the shifts noted and the sex differences cited?
2. Do you see further changes in either pattern likely? What kind? How and why?
3. Do you have any hypotheses or hunches about the impacts of death on sexism and ageism in the United States?
4. Would you rather have lived in 1900 than now? Discuss.
5. How do these data influence your thoughts about which sex struggles more to survive now? a century ago?

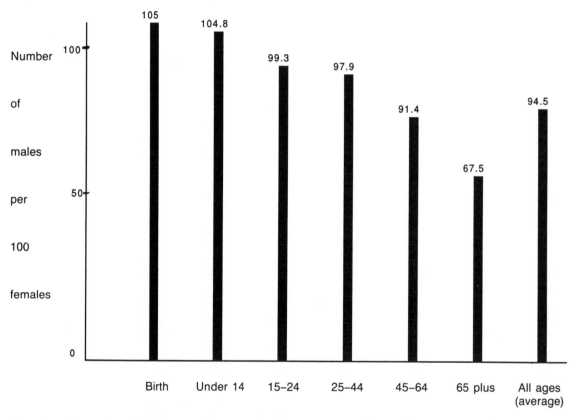

Note: According to the U.S. Census Bureau (1985), there are currently 6 million more females than males, with males outnumbering females until age 22. The widest gaps are under 5 years, where there are 9.1 million males to 8.7 females, while at 65 years and over, there are 16.7 million women to only 11.3 men. The ratio of unmarried women to available men widens dramatically after age 65. Medical studies have also indicated that the ratio of males to females conceived is 1.6 to 1.0.

Figure 2–1. Sex Differences in Age at Death Across the Life Span: Ratio of Males per 100 Females

	Shifting Age at Death: 1900 versus 1987	
	Percentage of Deaths Recorded	
Age Group	1900	1987
0–14	63	5
15–45	13	9
46–64	11	14
65 and over	13	72

Note: Recall that the population centers in each era were quite different, with only a handful of cities in the United States at the turn of the century. Most life-styles were agrarian, and both public health and job safety were minimal in 1900. It was said that a couple had to conceive eight times then to see three of their offspring survive to adulthood. Today the overwhelming majority of the populace is in cities and suburbs, and most workers are in light physical labor or service economy jobs. Those dying today are likeliest to be over sixty-five and in institutional settings. (Suggested by comment in Fulton, R. and Owen, G., 1987–88. "Death and society in Twentieth Century America," *Omega* 68: 379–395.)

2. Societal Mortality, Societal Belief

Goals To develop the relationship between mortality and belief systems and examine the part death plays in a society's orientation toward life.

Materials Large sheets of paper, markers and tape, chalkboard or overhead projector.

Time 30–40 minutes.

Procedures Subdivide the group into three sections, with one person in each assigned the role of recorder-reporter. Assign one of the following sets of societal characteristics to each group:

		Crude death rate	Infant mortality	Longest life span
Society A	Urban industrial	10:1,000	1%	70+
Society B	Agricultural, transitional	30:1,000	25	45 (approx.)
Society C	Primitive agricultural, hunting, gathering	50:1,000	35	30 or less

The facilitator should distinguish 50:1,000 death rate, 35% infant mortality, and life expectancy of less than 30 years as high mortality and 10:1,000 life expectancy of 70 or more years as low mortality rates.

Instruct each group to answer the following questions about its society in 20 minutes:

1. What age group is most likely to die in this country?
2. How much certainty is there in this society that a person is likely to live his or her entire life span?
3. What general type of belief system do you think would be used by this society to explain death?
4. What influence do you think death has on daily life and activities in this society?
5. What types of social, economic, and interpersonal relationships do you think are predominant in this society?

Each group makes a consensus summary or summary statement about its society, which the recorder-reporter will document and report to the total group. The consensus summary statements can be written out and displayed for all to see. The total group can then compare the statement and analyze elements that led to their conclusions.

Debriefing

1. Which society would you prefer to live in? to die in? Are they different?
2. How would life be different in each of the other societies?
3. What are the advantages of your society? disadvantages?
4. Does mortality have an effect on the belief systems of societies? What different combinations of data might have a different effect on your society?

---

3. Have a Heart

Goals

1. To provide a simulation of what a life-and-death decision might be like with only scarce resources available, one that parallels the everyday bioethical quandaries characterizing modern medical practice.
2. To enable participants to clarify what they value about their lives.
3. To experience problem solving when few absolutes prevail.
4. To examine what alterations in life-style a life-threatening illness can pose.

Setting

Room to accommodate circular seating for each member in a group.

Time

50 minutes minimum.

Procedures

1. Provide some background:

   Organ transplantation is not only a fairly common medical fact of life these days, but the coincident advances in medical diagnosis, care, and technology that have made transplantation possible ironically also have led to a greater shortage of donable organs relative to a greatly increased need. This is due in part to improvements in both screening and procurement, as well as in immunosuppression control. The American Council on Transplantation noted some alarming statistics over this past decade:

   1. In any given year 33,000 or more patients await a donor organ operation to lengthen and improve their lives.
   2. Nearly half this number die each year for want of a heart transplant.
   3. Estimates of organ shortfall indicate that only about one in seven possible donatable organs was in fact made available.

2. Form the participants into small groups of six to eight each.
3. Introduce the task:

   Each of you is a cardiac patient with a chronic cardiomyopathy (diseased heart muscle tissue) that is not curable except by transplanting a donor heart. Without this operation, you are not expected to live more than a few months and to be greatly disabled in the interim. While there are several significant matching considerations for being a candidate for transplantation, you have all been brought together because you have identical characteristics for a donor organ that is becoming available in the next 24 hours. We have no better, more equitable procedure for determining which one of you should become the chosen recipient than to have you as a group decide and select the fortunate one. That is your task.

   Here are the ground rules for your deliberations:

   a. You have to decide in the next 30 minutes.
   b. You cannot opt out; no self-sacrifices are allowed.
   c. You are to argue for your selection by building a case for yourself based on your actual life circumstances and history.
   d. You may argue for or against the inclusion of others.

4. You can share the following background information:
   a. Successful transplant recipients in the recent past were more likely to have been married, employed, near ideal weight, previously successful in coping with life crises, essentially flexible, optimistic, and conforming, with an active sectarian religious practice and a satisfying hobby prior to their illness.

b. Previous heart transplant recipients have sometimes had serious operative complications, including depressive illness, infrequent psychosis, immune system suppression leading to life-threatening infections, and numerous other side effects, including rejection of the donor heart by the recipient's body. Survival data range from 1 day to one man who lives still, over 20 years after his operation. Most have lived fewer than 5 years to date, but survival experience is lengthening annually.

5. Tell the groups to proceed (leader participation as a member is optional), but remind them that only 30 minutes is allotted for their deliberations. Give a warning when only 5 minutes are left, and adhere to the time limit.

6. At the end of the half-hour, tell them to stop and spend the next 20 or so minutes debriefing the activity. The main idea is to address the dynamics involved and the participants' reactions to their involvement. At the end, different groups' reactions can be solicited and compared, using the goals of the exercise to summarize.

Debriefing

1. What were the critical factors influencing your choice (medical, psychological, family-social, and others)?
2. Were any novel or compromise solutions proposed? If so, how were they dealt with?
3. What types of behaviors were evident, both in the course of arguing for one's selection and in the process of arriving at a consensus decision?
4. What values were highlighted and treated as significant factors in the course of the selection process? Why?
5. Note how often (or infrequently) mention of dying, death, and the possible vital consequences of your selection was made.
6. To what extent were you motivated to avoid making a decision, perhaps by choosing someone through some method of chance such as tossing a coin or drawing straws? Discuss the implications of such decision-making ploys.
7. To what extent did the group attempt to objectify an essentially subjective judgment by working out formula, point systems, and the like for rating candidates in some hierarchical manner? Was this effective? Why?
8. Discuss the overall impact of participating in such a decision-making process, particularly as a real task.
9. What particular reactions and insights have you gained from participating in a task, albeit simulated, where your personal values, goals, and interpersonal skills were so critical and in focus?

4. Giving It All Away

Goals

1. To assist participants in exploring and identifying feelings associated with an aspect of the dying process: giving up our prized possessions to people we love.
2. To provide a structure wherein participants can freely explore and discuss feelings of attachment and loss.

In our culture, few of us take the time to write our wills until we have reason to believe that our death is imminent. The assumption is commonly made that a will is not necessary until our elder years. Even then wills are often written in a language that does not adequately convey the personal feelings and meaning involved. This exercise is designed to assist participants in exploring the feelings that might be associated with this process of giving up our prized possessions and leaving them to the persons of our own choosing.

Materials

Paper and pencil for each participant (ten sheets per person); a small grill or heat-resistant container in which to burn the paper.

Time

Approximately 1½–2 hours.

Procedures

1. Begin by briefly restating the rationale. Then instruct each person to find a comfortable area in the room to work alone. Give each participant a pencil and ten sheets of paper.
2. Instruct participants to think about ten prized possessions each currently owns. Ask each to write the name of each possession on a separate sheet of paper. After each possession, ask each to write briefly what is most valued about the possession. For each possession, the participants are asked to choose some person they would most like to give that possession to. The participants are asked to choose a different person for each possession.
3. Ask the participants to form a close circle. Each participant in turn describes one of the possessions, what value it holds, who he or she would give it to, and why. After a participant has described one possession, he or she folds the sheet of paper and places it in the center of the circle. The turn is then passed to another participant. The same procedure is followed, until one by one, all ten possessions have been described by each person and placed in the center of the circle.
4. Place all the paper in a grill and set them to flame while participants watch silently.
5. Encourage participants to reflect silently for a few minutes on the meaning this experience has had for them.

Debriefing
1. What was this experience like for you?
2. What kind of feelings did you become aware of during this experience?
3. What was it like for you to describe your valued possessions?
4. What was it like to try to choose some person to give your possessions to?
5. What kind of feelings do you now have about your possessions? your loved ones?
6. What feelings do you now have about writing wills?

---

5. Burying Part of the Past

Goals
1. To assist participants in identifying thoughts, feelings, values, goals, and assumptions once held in the past but since dispatched.
2. To provide a framework wherein participants might recognize that the development of new dimensions of self involves the discarding of old viewpoints.
3. To promote exploration and discussion regarding the natural occurrence of change, loss, and separation as being an inherent part of development and change throughout life.

An important aspect of personal development is moving beyond old beliefs and attitudes that once influenced how we viewed ourselves and the world around us. Should we fail to do so by clinging to prior and outdated visions of ourselves, the development of valuable new dimensions of experience can be impeded. This exercise is designed to assist participants in identifying some of the beliefs, values, goals, and assumptions that were important at an earlier part of the life span but have changed in importance. By going through the ritual of "burying" past images of themselves, participants are assisted in exploring how loss and separation are a natural part of the developmental process and how loss sets the stage for continued creative discovery.

Materials
Each participant is asked to bring a photograph of himself or herself taken several years in the past. If pictures are not available, the leader could provide paper and pen to each participant and ask each to draw a rough sketch of how he or she looked several years ago.

Time
Approximately 1 hour.

Procedures
1. Ask each participant to have available a picture of himself or herself taken several years ago. If pictures are not available, each participant is asked to draw a likeness as if the picture was a snapshot from the past.

2. Ask participants individually to take a close look at their own picture and try to remember vividly what their life experience was like then.
3. Ask each participant to write their responses to the following:
    a. "When I was that age, three things I was excited about were . . ."
    b. "When I was that age, three things I was afraid of were . . ."
    c. "When I was that age, three things I felt proud of were . . ."
    d. "When I was that age, three goals I had were . . ."
4. Ask each participant to go back over the responses and check those that no longer fit. Next, they write their checked responses on the back of their pictures.
5. All the participants form a close circle. (If there are more than seven or eight present, form circles of four or more members in roughly equal-sized groupings.) Each person, in turn, is invited to place his or her picture face down in the center of the circle and to say "good-bye" to the parts from the past that no longer fit, to "bury" them.
6. After participants have placed their pictures in the circle, have them close their eyes and reflect on the various meanings this experience may have had for them.

Debriefing

1. What was this experience like for you?
2. What parts from your past still fit for you?
3. What was it like for you to say goodbye to feelings and thoughts from the past?
4. What current beliefs, goals, and values do you imagine might change in the coming years? Which are likely to remain the same?
5. Was there a single event that led to real transformation from that phase of how you were? Elaborate.
6. How do these changes and adaptations parallel others in your prior or subsequent years?

Those who wish may retrieve their picture.

---

6. Farewell, Snoopy

Goals

1. To consider nonhuman loss and the bereavement experience it can engender.
2. To acknowledge the very personal and individual nature of grief reactions.
3. To examine the range and role of preparatory or anticipatory grief in human experience.
4. To look at some aspects of "assisted death."

Setting

The activity is best undertaken in small groups of about four or five.

Materials   Copy of the "Dear Becky" letter that follows and a pen or pencil for each participant.

Time   45 minutes.

Procedures   1. Explain the goals of the activity in general terms to the group. Then give each participant a copy of the letter that follows to read to themselves quietly.
                       2. After reading it, each person turns the sheet over and spends about 10 minutes writing responses to these queries which can be copied or displayed:
                          a. Do you have (or have you had) a dog, cat, or other domestic pet? If yes, write their name(s). Is the pet still living?
                          b. If you have lost a pet, how, when, and what age were you at the time of death(s)?
                          c. What are your feelings about "putting a pet to sleep"?
                       3. The subgroups then discuss the questions listed under "Debriefing." They should begin by selecting a group reporter who can take notes and summarize their particular small group's discussion for the whole group.

Variations   Participants can be asked to write a similar letter to a good friend notifying them of the death and/or loss of their own pet as it happened or might occur (if the pet is still alive or the writer has never been a pet owner). This can be done instead of reading the sample here or after reading it and either before or after debriefing in small groups.

Debriefing   1. How does the loss and/or death of a pet compare with human loss in your bereavement experience?
                       2. What did you experience in recalling your own pet's demise? If you are a current pet owner, what do you feel in anticipation of such a loss?
                       3. What is your belief about "afterlife" for pets?
                       4. Does the "putting to sleep" of a pet compare at all to euthanasia with people? How so or not?
                       5. How important to their grief work is the developmental level and capability of the person at the time of pet loss? to their subsequent grief experiences?
                       6. How do you view the loss of a pet for a person living alone? Is it likely to have different consequences? How?
                       7. What are your thoughts about replacing a pet?

"Dear Becky Letter"

Dear Becky:

Yesterday the worst thing happened! We had to have Snoopy put to sleep! I'm so depressed and lonely, and he's only been gone for 17½ hours.

My cute little pal for eight years, my constant and faithful buddy since grade school is gone now. I said "Goodbye" to him, but he was so sick I don't know if he even heard me or could care for anything but his poor, painful body. The vet said it was congestive heart failure that did him in. He was having trouble even breathing, let alone getting around to eat or walk.

Remember how he used to love to chase squirrels and to fetch the Frisbee and how good he was at jumping and catching it in the air? Gosh, he was fun, and a really great dog! I dont' think I'll get over this soon. I sure can't imagine any other dog ever taking his place?

I've been mostly crying and hiding out so nobody can see how bummed out I am. If you were here, at least I'd know you understood, 'cause I recall how we were when you found out about Sylvia getting hit by a car when she was barely more than a kitten. I can't write any more now. Wish you were here for me.

Love,
Franny

---

7. Fleeting Time

Goals

1. To heighten individuals' awareness of the finiteness of the time allotted them.
2. To permit participants to examine their manner of coping with limited time.
3. To permit people to examine their manner of coping with constraints upon their involvement with persons and tasks.
4. To permit an examination of their manner of coping with arbitrary events.

Arbitrary and unexpected termination of participants' activities provides a parallel to the realization that one's death is pending.

Materials

An alarm clock or timer with a bell or buzzer for each group or, if the number of participants is smaller than ten, one timer for each person; masking tape; felt-tip pens; extra chairs arranged facing walls away from the central work area.

Time

Adaptable to the time available but at least 60 minutes.

Procedures

Ask each participant (for ten or fewer) to bring a timer with an alarm bell or buzzer or a similar self-powered alarm clock (or provide one for each group or person). Clearly print the name of each participant on a piece of masking tape and place each piece of tape on the front of a separate clock or timer. Ask each participant to note which clock is his or hers. Then randomly set each alarm to go off at a different time during the ensuing session or workshop period. Optimal impact is obtained when alarms on one or two clocks are not set at all. Clocks should be set far enough apart that all participants know when theirs has rung and far enough from the participants that they cannot see the time for which the alarm is set, perhaps under their seat or desk. Tell participants that when an alarm goes off, they must immediately stop what they are doing, move to a chair facing the wall, and remain there until further notification. Reconvene the total group 20–30 minutes before the end of the session for debriefing.

The exercise is most effective when superimposed upon other activities that require maximal participant involvement. For instance, it might best be employed in conjunction with another structured experience, an active group discussion, or a planning task in which all individuals are engaged. It is least effective when undertaken during a presentation by the facilitator or any one member of the group.

Variations

Participants can be asked how the awareness that they might have to disengage affected their involvement in the task. They might then be asked how they would have behaved differently had they known *when* they would be forced to stop.

Expressions of frustration, helplessness, anger (often directed toward the facilitator), and eventual detachment are common in reaction to this exercise. As these feelings are expressed, parallels can be drawn gently to receiving the diagnosis of a terminal illness or the occurrence of an incapacitating injury. This awareness often leads to a degree of resolution on the part of some participants to live life more fully while there is the opportunity.

Debriefing

Discussion of this experience can include exploration of participants' reactions to the following:

- The interruption
- Its arbitrariness
- Its unexpectedness
- Being excluded from the task
- Being isolated from other participants
- Being left behind as others are forced to leave the task
- The control exercised by the facilitator
- The realization that some participants' alarms never sounded

---

8. Time Runs Out

Goals

1. To increase sensitivity to the fact that loss and death can occur without warning.
2. To develop increased awareness of the finiteness of time we have available in our lives.
3. To assist participants in identifying feelings associated with loss and change.

Often we take for granted the amount of time we have available to us in our lives, as if we have all the time in the world. A personal tragedy or a near-fatal accident can shock us into awareness that our time is indeed limited. This awareness can often serve to motivate us to engage our energies more fully in living.

Materials

1. An alarm clock.
2. Some type of construction material for each participant, such as construction paper, cardboard and masking tape, or matchsticks and glue.
3. Slips of paper to identify the name of each participant and a container in which to place these.
4. Sheets of paper listing one of the following instructions.
   a. "Your time has run out. All construction materials will be taken from you immediately. Sit quietly for the remainder of the period." (Approximately one-fourth of instruction sheets contain this instruction.)

b. "You have suffered a serious setback. Half of your construction materials will be taken from you immediately." (Approximately one-fourth of instruction sheets contain this instruction.)

c. "You have been diagnosed with a terminal illness. You have only 2 remaining minutes to complete your project." (Approximately one-fourth of instruction sheets contain this instruction.)

d. "Due to advancing age, you can no longer complete the project you chose initially. Lower your expectations and choose another project." (Approximately one-fourth of instruction sheets contain this instruction.)

The leader folds sheets and places them in random order in a pile (one sheet for each participant). Throughout the exercise these instructions are referred to as "fate" instructions."

Time 1½ hours.

Procedures This exercise is designed to stimulate exploration, discussion, and increased awareness about the arbitrary nature of time. In the exercise, the participants work on a project of their own creation for 30 minutes. During this 30-minute period, an alarm clock is arranged to ring at random intervals. Each time the alarm rings, one of the particpant's names is randomly drawn from a container. The participant is then required to face one of four possible consequences:

1. To stop working on the project immediately.
2. To lose half of his or her construction materials.
3. To have only 2 remaining minutes to complete the project.
4. To choose another project task.

By the end of the 30-minute period, at least three-quarters of the participants will have to face a "consequence" that will significantly affect their ability to complete their project as initially planned. Assist the participants in discussing parallels between this exercise and real-life experiences associated with death, loss and aging.

1. Give each participant some construction material with the following instruction:

   During the next 30 minutes, each of you will have the opportunity to make something creative out of the construction material I've just given to you. Your specific task will be to make something that represents a part of yourself that you are proud of. Reflect for a few moments and then choose some specific thing you could make that would represent some aspect of yourself that you feel good about. For example, if you are proud of your ability to make friends, you might make something from the construction materials that symbolizes friendship.

Do the very best job you can during this next 30 minutes. During this work period, work silently. At random intervals during this period, this alarm clock will be set to ring. Each time it rings, I will randomly draw one of your names from this container. Then I will randomly select a specific instruction for you to follow from this other pile. These instructions are called "fate instructions." When the alarm clock rings, continue to work silently on your project unless I come and tap you on the shoulder. If you are tapped on the shoulder, you will be given your specific fate instructions to follow. Please follow these fate instructions and proceed silently.

2. Each participant must announce to the others his or her chosen construction project. Then participants begin working.
3. Set the alarm clock to ring at random intervals. During the 30-minute work period, arrange for the alarm clock to ring enough times to draw the names of at least three or four of the participants. When the alarm clock rings, randomly draw one of the participant's names from the container and randomly select one of the fate instruction sheets. Silently read the fate instructions and then give the instruction sheet to the selected participant after first tapping that participant on the shoulder. For example, for the fate instruction sheet stating "Your time has run out. All construction materials will be taken from you immediately. Sit quietly for the remainder of the period," take the instructions to the selected participant, show the instructions, and silently take the construction materials from the participant.
4. Reset the alarm clock to ring at some random work period. Again, it is suggested that the leader set the alarm clock so that it will ring enough times to draw the names of at least three to four of the participants.
5. After 30 minutes reconvene the whole group.

Debriefing

Begin the debriefing procedure by asking participants to show and describe how much they were able to complete of their individual construction projects. This will encourage the open expression of feelings from the participants. Some possible questions for use in discussing the experience follow:

1. What was this experience like for you?
2. What kind of feelings were stirred up inside you each time the alarm clock rang? when you were tapped on the shoulder? when you read your instructions? as you followed your instructions?
3. What kind of reactions did you have toward the leader? toward other participants?

4. Which fate instructions do you believe were most difficult to follow? Why?
5. How might the other participants have assisted you in dealing with your fate instructions if they had been given the opportunity?
6. How do you feel about the overall quality of your work on your construction project? How might you have improved the quality of your work?
7. For those of you who experienced setbacks or who were cut short of time, what were your reactions? How did you deal with these reactions?
8. What are some ways the feelings stirred up in this experience for you might be similar or dissimilar to the feelings a person might have toward some actual experiences such as death, loss, and aging?

In order to extend the learning parallel between this simulated exercise and death, close the exercise by requesting that all participants in turn bring their created projects to the center of the room, place the project on the floor, and return to be seated in the circle. As each person returns, perform a ritual of covering the created project with a box or blanket and then destroying the remains of it. Explain that each project will be destroyed and each participant has the option of looking on or turning away. After destroying each project, debrief this part of the exercise with the following questions:

1. What was it like for you to give up your project? to hear that it had to be destroyed?
2. When you learned your project was to be destroyed, what thoughts did you have about whether to watch or turn your head away? How did you decide which to do?
3. What kind of feelings did you then have about seeing your project destroyed? What feelings came later?
4. What kind of feelings did you have about seeing others' projects destroyed?
5. What kind of learning did this part of the experience provide you?

9. My Body: Now and Then

Goals

1. To stimulate thought and exploration about a significant change that occurs through life as people approach death: the change in body strength, resilience, and form.
2. To assist individuals in identifying significant aspects of their body image and exploring their feelings and attitudes about their changing bodies.

Discussing death and dying necessarily encompasses discussing the countless variety of losses that death signifies. Obviously important losses occur in our bodies due to the aging process and ultimately the loss of the body itself through death. This exercise is designed to stimulate thinking about some of the changes and losses associated with our bodies as we approach death.

Materials
Paper and pencil for each participant.

Time
Approximately 45 minutes.

Procedures
1. Present a brief rationale to the group for the exercise.
2. Instruct each participant to draw three pictures of his or her body:

Picture 1: A picture of how they look today. Participants are asked to emphasize or exaggerate the area of their body they are proudest of.

Picture 2: A picture of how they looked at a much younger age. Participants are asked to emphasize or exaggerate the area of the body they are proudest of.

Picture 3: A picture of how they imagine they will look as they approach death. Participants should pay special attention to the body area they are currently proudest of.

Variations
Use of this option depends on the maturity level of the participants and the trust level the group has formed. Participants can be asked to draw a picture of their bodies at the moment of death. They are also asked to give special attention to the body part they currently are proudest of.

Debriefing
1. What kind of changes occurred to the body part you were proudest of? How did you feel about these changes?
2. Did other parts of your body change in importance as you grew older? Did some parts become more important?
3. As your body changed and continues to change, what are or might be some of the life-style adaptations you have made or may make?
4. Now that you completed this exercise, how do you feel about your body?
5. What are the differences between aging and dying? Should they be equated?

These questions can be discussed if the procedure variation was utilized:

1. What was it like for you to imagine your body at the moment of death? What kind of feelings did this stir up?
2. Were you able to complete the picture? If so, what were you thinking as you completed it? If not, what prevented you?

10. Wrinkles of Time

Goals

1. To sensitize individuals to the reality of the aging process and the inevitability of old age.
2. To elicit participants' attitudes and feelings about old age.
3. To heighten participants' appreciation of their current level of vitality and mobility.
4. To incorporate current physical accommodations into projected future appearance.

Materials

Several small mirrors or access to a large mirror (as in a dressing room); a place to apply and remove makeup; talcum powder; several different shades of moist makeup base; makeup remover; brown eyebrow pencil (blunt ended); ball of string or twine; any makeup the person now uses; a covering, such as an old shirt, to wear while makeup is being applied; cold cream (for removing makeup). Nonallergenic products should be used.

Time

1½ hours.

Procedures

1. Instruct participants to work in pairs, selecting a partner with whom they are relatively comfortable. Using the powder, makeup base, and eyebrow pencil, each will spend 15 minutes making up the face and hair of their partner to simulate a person ten to twenty years older. The most potent effect is obtained by first applying the makeup base over the entire face and neck and then using the eyebrow pencil to outline wrinkles and provide shading. The contours of the individual's own smile and frown wrinkles and the photograph of the face of an elderly person serve as guides for the makeup process.

    The talcum powder is used to highlight shading on the face and neck and to whiten head and facial hair if that person intends to let hair color change remain. The emotional impact of viewing oneself upon completion of this process is commensurate with the time and effort the partner devotes to making up the individual. Hence, careful attention to the process is encouraged. The facilitator may serve as a technical adviser to participants throughout the process. When this part of the makeup process has been completed, participants are directed to spend a few minutes viewing themselves in the mirror and paying attention to their reactions. If the person currently uses makeup and/or hair color and anticipates continued use, that additional makeup accommodation should be applied now. Again, instruct participants to view themselves in the mirror and note their reactions. At this time, goals 1–4 might be addressed, or proceed to the next part of the activity and postpone all discussion until the end.

2. Each participant cuts approximately 3 feet of string from the roll of twine. They tie their right and left leg together at the ankles such that there are about 8–12 inches of string between their two feet. They are directed to mill around the room, interacting with one another as if at a social gathering. Approximately 15 minutes should be allowed for this step. Then participants are called together to discuss the experience.

Participants should be told prior to the session that they will be asked to remove makeup and may wish to reapply their own makeup later and that there is the possibility that hair will be altered. Make sure that facilities and time are available to clean up after the session.

It is essential for the leader to have already experienced the process of being made up and of making up another individual so he or she can better anticipate participants' reactions to the exercise and more effectively debrief them. It is, in fact, helpful if the leader has himself or herself made up at the beginning of this session so that he or she may serve as a model of the end product and be free to provide technical assistance throughout the process.

Depending upon the shared history and the trust level within the group, it might be constructive for the facilitator to demonstrate the makeup process with a member of the group, particularly if there has been no precedent established for touching among group members. Through matter-of-fact attention to the makeup task, the leader can establish an atmosphere in which anxiety about touching and being touched is minimized.

It is suggested that as participants view themselves in the mirror and as they interact at the social gathering, they monitor (though not necessarily alter) their laughter and joking. Laughter can be a means of diffusing the anxiety associated with altered appearance and mobility and can detract from the impact of the experience unless participants are aware of the function it is serving.

Variation

The facilitator may wish to have an instant camera and film available to take pictures of any participants who care to have a picture of themselves.

Debriefing

1. What was your first reaction upon seeing yourself in the mirror?
2. What sort of thoughts come to mind as you look at yourself in the future?
3. How do you feel about yourself? about the others?
4. Do you feel more or less valuable? energetic? productive? confident? involved? capable?
5. Did you adjust the appearance your partner gave you?
6. Will you begin or continue to use makeup, hair color, or other accommodation to adjust the natural effects of aging? Why or why not?

7. What other accommodations can or might you make for a changing body?
8. How does it feel to have your mobility impaired?
9. How does it feel to have your freedom limited? your choices reduced?
10. In what ways do these changes affect the way you think about yourself?
11. With the binding removed, how does it feel to have your agility returned?
12. How does your experience with this exercise apply to persons whose bodies may be changing prematurely due to disease, injury, or illness?

---

11. Another View

Goals

1. To give individuals who have experienced losses another perspective on loss.
2. To depict loss experience as part of a process, continuum, and framework that can lead to personal growth.
3. To utilize nonverbal methods for fantasy exploration, paving the way for creativity and reintegration.

Materials

Pastels or soft crayons and large sheets of paper for each participant.

Time

2–3 hours.

Procedures

1. Participants select a partner who, if possible, they do not know. For 10 minutes, they exchange names, briefly relate a particular loss, and share something positive related to the present or the future. Examples are something good to eat, a rewarding activity, someone they love.
2. Pairs join together with another dyad to become groups of four. Each member of the original dyad introduces the partner to the others in the small group. The four interact by relating their current experience, focusing on feelings, insights, physical sensations, and whatever else they wish.
3. Distribute paper and drawing materials and tell the group:

   Draw three pictures in any way you choose. Skill is irrelevant. You will have approximately 15 minutes for each picture. The first drawing is about you and your world before your loss. The second drawing is about you and your world in the present. The third is a possible future. If there is any bright place, try to include anyone or anything you feel will help you reach that place. If for now there is no bright place, see if there is anyone or anything that can help you in your darkness and incorporate that person or thing.

4. Participants next share their pictures with their original group of four. After about 15 minutes, ask them to select one they are willing to share with the whole group. Within the context of a supportive environment, group discussion should follow.

Debriefing
1. How did you feel as you drew each picture?
2. Did you learn anything about yourself as you were drawing?
3. In what ways are the pictures alike?
4. What do you see as the role of the future from your picture?
5. Did others see things in your pictures you were not aware of?
6. Was it difficult to show your pictures to others?
7. Were your pictures in any way similar to those of others?
8. How did you feel about seeing others' pictures?
9. How did the first part of the exercise relate to the rest?
10. Do you see your loss on a continuum? Do you view others' pictures and loss as part of a continuum?

12. Life versus Death

Goals
1. To enable individuals to reflect on their particular associations to death and dying and life and living.
2. To provide a minimal structure for facilitating discussion.

Through the use of a drawing activity, this exercise makes possible the surfacing of some perceptual dimensions that might not be revealed in a more formal method. Because of the ambiguous nature of the drawings, participants are able to express and explore their feelings about dying and living from both the activity of drawing and from interpreting the drawings of others.

Materials
Two sheets of paper for each participant; crayons or pencils. One sheet should be titled "I'm Living" and the other "I'm Dying."

Time
50 minutes.

Procedures
1. Instruct participants to sit in a circle. In large groups (over fifteen), two circles could be formed.
2. Give each participant a sheet of blank paper with "I'm Dying" written at the top and provide these instructions:

Take a few moments and reflect. Then draw a picture that shows what you would feel if you fully knew you were dying soon. The picture you draw does not have to be highly artistic or realistic, only an expression of what you feel.

Allow 10–15 minutes for each person to complete the picture.

3. Give each participant another sheet of paper with the title: "I'm Living":

   Take a few moments again and reflect. Then draw a picture that shows what you feel when you fully know you are living.

   Allow 10–15 minutes for each person to complete drawing.

4. Ask each person in turn to share his or her drawings of "I'm Dying" and "I'm Living" with the rest of the group, describing what is portrayed in the drawings. Or ask participants to shuffle and redistribute the drawings to others in the group. Each person then describes what she or he sees in the drawing held. An advantage of this second method is that it allows the artist to remain anonymous.

Variations and Debriefing

1. As each person describes what he or she sees in the pictures, a master list can be made on newsprint or board, noting everything associated with the two terms. This could serve to organize and generate further discussion.

2. The pictures could be replaced by a word instruction. Ask each learner to take a blank sheet of paper and to write the words "Death is . . ." on the top of the page on one side. They are to complete the stem by writing as many thoughts as come to mind in 3–5 minutes but stopping at the bottom of the side if time is not up. Then they turn the sheet over and write at the top of the second side "Life is . . . " and take an equal amount of time to complete the thought on the rest of that side. Debriefing this variation can be done in pairs or small groups as well, focusing on the comparisons and contrasts in the responses and also looking at the similarities or differences between the two sides of the pages. This variation and its debriefing take at least a half-hour.

3. Limit the last set of instructions to a single response. The final products can then be collected and copied on a single side each in some fairly reasonable order to produce a large, free-form "poem." Copy it and distribute it later to the group for discussion. It can yield some unique compositions, gives all a sense of equal contribution, and lead to interesting group discussion.

In all of these approaches, the objective is to allow the production of free, open-ended descriptions for sharing and examining reactions. The frequent use of both metaphor and simile that occurs in dealing with the difficulty posed by the task is an important part of the process. Often the main ways of defining these terms are by negating some living process or by viewing them merely as stark opposites. Fruitful debate and elaboration of meaning can occur as a result of using this line of inquiry.

---

13. Activities Contraction Brainstorm

Goals

1. To acquaint individuals with the kinds of daily decisions faced by many terminally ill persons.
2. To sensitize individuals to the restricted activities available to those who are confined to bed with a terminal illness.
3. To serve as a stimulus for discussing various aspects of the dying process.

   Through a brainstorming procedure, participants are stimulated to identify the typical day-to-day activities and decisions the terminally ill must relinquish due to health, diminished mobility, and restricted resources.

Materials   On a large sheet of paper or on a chalkboard, draw the following:

Time   1 hour.

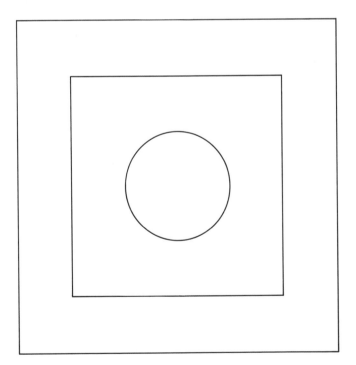

Procedures

1. Request participants to form a semicircle of chairs around the blackboard and then explain the activity:

   The outer square represents all activities you can do and decisions you can make on an average day when you are feeling totally rested and healthy. What I would like you to do is to think now of items for this category. Call them out, and I will write them down. We're interested in a quantity of good ideas, not determining their merit as yet.

   If there is hesitation, provide suggestions: when to wake up, what to wear, what to eat, when to leave for work, getting the kids off to school, and so on. Encourage participants by joining in yourself. Write the activities and decisions inside the square or beside it with an arrow to the appropriate space. Try to avoid getting mired in details of the entire day; a sample will do. Gently encourage each person to participate.

2. Move on to the inner square:

   The inner sqaure represents all activities you can do and decisions you can make when you are able to move freely about but are sick with a terminal illness. Which of the things we have in the outer square can we copy into this inner square? Which are no longer possible or plausible for whatever reason?

   Take time to encourage participants to verbalize why some activities or decisions might not be possible in the second box.

3. Finally, say:

   The inner circle represents all activities you can do and all decisions you can make when you are confined to bed with a terminal illness. We will have to use our imaginations a little bit because this is not an easy task. Which activities can we copy into the inner circle?

Variations

This exercise can also be done using a three-level funnel figure. Depending on the focus of the group participants, other scenarios may be more appropriate, such as specific illnesses, prior stroke, AIDS, effects of treatment, disability, or not being able to work.

Debriefing

1. How easy was it for you to imagine the kinds of activities and decisions a terminally ill person might make?
2. Which activities and decisions would be most difficult for you to give up?
3. Recall the last time you were confined to bed. How did you handle being confined to bed with an illness or injury that was not terminal, such as the flu? How might you handle being confined to bed with a terminal illness? What might you want from your loved ones to assist you in handling this kind of situation?

14. Attending Your Own Funeral

Goals

1. To assist individuals in clarifying feelings and values related to funerals, specifically, their own funerals.
2. To acquaint individuals with the finality of their own deaths.
3. To offer individuals an opportunity to evaluate certain aspects of their lives.

Through guided fantasy, participants are conducted through the experience of their own funerals. They thereby review and evaluate aspects of their life, including the quality of interpersonal relationships.

Materials

A room in which participants can lie comfortably on their backs not touching other participants.

Time

1–1½ hours.

Procedures

Instructions for the guided fantasy are as follows:

Those of you who wear contact lenses might want to remove them, as I will be asking to have your eyes closed for a while. Now lie on your back, legs uncrossed, and make yourself as comfortable as you can. Close your eyes, and let all the events and worries of the day roll around in your mind. (pause) And when you're ready, leave all those thoughts behind and just appreciate how peaceful and relaxed you feel. Pay attention to those places where you feel tense, and let those parts of your body relax. (pause) Take a deep breath, hold it and let it out slowly.

You are in complete control of your own imagination now, so just follow along with what I am saying as long as you are willing. *

Now let your body go. Imagine that the life is gone out of it. Do not speak or move.

Imagine that you have died. Your body is passive, lifeless, useless. Your body is discarded. Your funeral is about to take place.

You are now going to your own funeral.

Look at the people who have come to your funeral. What do they feel? (pause) How do they look at your body? Do they need consolation? (pause) Are they happy to be alive? Would they like to be dead? What are their emotions? (pause)

Look at the people coming to say a last goodbye to this discarded body. Look at each of them. Is there one among them to

---

* From this point on, the fantasy is adapted from Laura Huxley, *You are not the target* (New York: Farrar, Straus and Giroux, 1963). Reprinted with permission.

whom you would like to say something, to explain something, to express a certain feeling? (pause) You cannot do it. Without your power of speech, of writing, of moving—without your body you can do nothing.

Look again at the people who attend your funeral. What would you like to say to each of them, if you could speak? (pause) How would you express yourself to this or that person, if you had a body? (pause)

Do you have a problem that has been difficult to solve? Do you have a decision that has been difficult to make? (pause) Your problem, your decision might become clearer at this moment.

Did you look at the flowers the people sent you? What kind are they? How many are there? Did the people try to suit the preferences of the person your were? Or did they only do what they thought they ought to do?

Is anyone giving the eulogy? What is he or she saying? (pause) Does it seem to you sensible, reasonably true to you and your life?

Is there music? Has someone chosen it who knew what you liked, what you would prefer?

Now turn your attention to the person whom you disliked . . . or who irritated or repelled you more than any other in your life. (pause) Is there anything you want to say to that person? (pause)

Say it (in your imagination).

And now look at the one or ones you love the most, at the one or ones to whom you are most grateful. (pause) (In your imagination) say whatever you . . . feel like saying . . .

This is your last party. Speak to everyone there, tell them all about yourself, about your mistakes and your suffering (pause), about your love and your longings (pause). No longer do you need to protect yourself, no longer do you need to hide behind a wall or a suit of armor. It is your last party: you can explode, you can be miserable or pitiful, insignificant or despicable. At your funeral you can be yourself. (pause)

And now it is over. Come back to your living body.

Acknowledge it and respect it. Feel the life flowing in it. Feel your heart beat. Notice your breathing.

When you're ready, let your attention come back to this room. Now I'm going to count backwards slowly from 5 to 1. When I reach 1, I want you to open your eyes and you will feel alert and rested. Okay. 5 . . . 4 . . . 3 . . . 2 . . . 1. Open your eyes (pause), sit up, and look around you."

Some individuals are able to fantasize better than others. Reassure participants that it is all right if they experience difficulty in placing themselves into the fantasy.

In processing the guided fantasy, attend to underreaction as well as overreaction on the part of the participants. Not only does fantasy focus the individual inward, but also the content of this fantasy emphasizes the ultimate aloneness of each individual. It becomes all the more important, then, to know the state of mind in which each participant leaves this experience.

Debriefing

Before a fantasy is debriefed, it is wise to communicate to the participants some reassurance and some guidelines for constructive processing of individual fantasies:

> *Your fantasy is strictly yours to keep or to share as you please. Feel no pressure to disclose your fantasy. If you choose to share it with the group, you may do so in part or in full.*
>
> *If your fantasy involves another person, these are your imaginings about the relationship between you and that other person. Should you decide to share your fantasy with that person, it might provide a valuable springboard from which to discuss your feelings and thoughts with each other.* [This guideline mitigates against individuals' viewing their fantasies as absolute truth rather than as suggestion. It also places emphasis upon the *interaction* highlighted by the fantasy, as opposed to assigning responsibility, guilt or blame for the fantasy to one party or the other.]

After such reassurance, employ the following debriefing questions:

1. What was the experience like for you?
2. Would you like to share any part of your fantasy?
3. Was there any part of your fantasy that was especially meaningful to you?
4. Did you discover anything about your preferences regarding your own funeral?
5. Did anything about the way you are living your life become clearer to you?
6. Did you experience any realizations about persons in your life? about your relationships in general?
7. Did you discover any unfinished business that you might like to pursue at this time?

---

15. Trip to the Cemetery

Goals

1. To expose individuals to the inevitability of their own deaths.
2. To invite participants to confront the mortality and ultimate disposition of their bodies.
3. To permit them to make a symbolic statement about their uniqueness.

Setting	A moderately large cemetery with varied terrain and vegetation.
Time	2–3 hours
Procedure	**Preparation**

It is recommended that this exercise be combined with exercise 17, "Eulogy," and/or exercise 24, "Planning the Last Day." If this is done participants should have written their own eulogies prior to the trip to the cemetery and should have these in hand during the visit.

Secure permission for the visit from the cemetery management prior to the trip.

Instruct participants to meet at the cemetery at a designated time and place. It is suggested that each participant come alone in order to permit anticipatory thoughts and feelings about the experience to emerge with minimal intrusion and diffusion.

Instructions

After all participants have arrived, present the group with the following guidelines:

> Take the next 30 minutes to be alone and explore the grounds of the cemetery. Keep the quiet; give yourself a chance to reflect and respect the privacy of other individuals and groups, whether fellow participants or strangers. Allow yourself to pursue any feelings, thoughts, or images that come to mind. Do not push them away; experience them fully.
>
> During your walk, find a spot that especially appeals to you and in which you feel particularly comfortable. Spend a few minutes in that place, attending to how it feels to sit there and thinking about how you are represented by the place you have selected.
>
> After you have taken some time to explore the grounds and to spend some time in a special spot of your choosing, return here [to the designated meeting place], and we will talk for a few minutes before moving on to the next part of the experience.

When participants reconvene, some minimal (no more than 5–10 minutes) discussion is appropriate. The objective is simply to touch base with participants and make a cursory determination of how each is being affected by the experience thus far.

Participants remain together for the next portion of the visit. Each participant in turn leads the group to the spot he or she has selected as being of special importance. The participant who has selected that spot takes a few moments to share why that place was selected and in what ways it reflects him or her. If the eulogy is included in this exercise, the participant then gives his or her own eulogy to another participant to read.

The group moves in turn to the place selected by each participant, giving every person the opportunity to describe the significance of that spot and to hear his or her own eulogy read aloud by another individual of the participant's choosing.

Although it is neither realistic nor desirable to prevent participants from sharing their reactions as they move one place to the next, extensive debriefing of this activity should be reserved until the group has visited each participant's place in the cemetery.

Debriefing

The trip to the cemetery tends to promote introspection, a sense of quietness, and an appreciation of one's ultimate aloneness. The result is that there might exist among the participants a disinclination to discuss the experience in detail and a preference for silent reflection within the supportive context of the group. Such withdrawal should not be viewed as undesirable, though some discussion should be encouraged. Participants should be *offered* the opportunity to articulate their reactions. Provide this opportunity by respecting participants' rights to privacy, maintaining an atmosphere of warmth and safety, validating the full range of participant reactions, modeling appropriate self-disclosure, and remaining attentive and responsive to individuals' needs.

The following are some of the reactions that might be anticipated:

- Memories of deaths and funerals of loved ones.
- Anticipation of the reactions of loved ones to the participant's death.
- Meditation upon the infiniteness of a final resting place.
- Sadness about one's own death or the deaths of others.
- Fear or anxiety about one's own death or the deaths of others.
- Contemplation of one's body—its finiteness, its disposition.
- Speculation about mortality and immortality.
- Reflection upon one's life and that which has lent it meaning.

---

16. Notice of My Dying

Goals

1. To experience planning life with a specific identified end.
2. To examine life as it is lived in contrast to "planned" life.
3. To examine life as told through obituary statistics.
4. To personalize funeral planning.

This exercise is designed to provide the participant with an opportunity for examination and reflection of his or her own life and some element of control over the environment, relationships, and activities at its end and immediately following.

Materials

Paper and pens or pencils.

Time   1–1½ hours.

Procedures   Inform the participants:

You have a terminal illness that cannot be cured by surgery, medication, or other treatment. You have been told you have approximately 1 year to live. Individually answer the following questions after giving some thought to each:

1. *How do you intend to spend the last year of your life? Be as specific as you can, including people, places, activities. [Allow about 15 minutes].*
2. *Write your own obituary notice. Include:*
   a. *The usual vital statistics found in an obituary such as name, age, marital status and relatives.*
   b. *Jobs you've had and organizations you have belonged to, with positions you have held in them.*
   c. *Notable contributions you have made to the community.*
   d. *Your wishes for memorial tributes from friends.*
   e. *Would you include a picture? What kind? [Allow another 10–15 minutes.]*
3. *Plan you own funeral, including type of visitation and funeral, music selections, flowers, readings, and type of disposition (burial, cremation, or entombment). Be specific in identifying these and include them if possible. [Allow about 30 minutes.]*

Debriefing

1. Did you imagine yourself with a specific illness? What were the physical and mental effects?
2. Did the effects of illness influence your planning?
3. Who and what did you include in your last year?
4. Was this a radical change from the way you now live? If so, why don't you make these changes now?
5. What things, other than those included in your obituary notice, would you want others to know about you?
6. What items in the obituary notice do you see as most significant? least significant? Why?
7. Explain why you chose the specific parts of your funeral. What significance do these elements have to you? to others who would be present at your funeral?
8. What will those at your funeral do immediately afterward?
9. What part of this exercise was easiest? most difficult?
10. Have you already thought about any of these things? communicated them to others?
11. Did your feelings change from the beginning of this exercise to the end? In what way?

17. Eulogy

Goals

1. To invite individuals to confront the inevitability that their lives will end.
2. To provide people with a perspective from which to view the whole of their lives.
3. To permit individuals to preview the feelings they might experience about themselves in looking back on their lives.
4. To offer people an opportunity to examine any discrepancies between their values, goals, and priorities and the way they currently conduct their lives. By means of constructing the story of one's life and hearing that story read by another individual, the participant is able to obtain a broader perspective of self, the past, present, and future.

Materials

Paper and pencils.

Time

25 minutes and 5 additional minutes per participant.

Procedures

1. Begin the exercise with the following instructions:

   Common definitions of the term eulogy *regard it as a laudatory statement, a message of praise usually honoring a special guest at a social function or at the time of demise. Your task is to write the eulogy that you wish it were possible and realistic to have delivered about you at your funeral. The eulogy is to be distinguished from an obituary that appears in the newspaper as notification of your death. Don't write the eulogy that could be delivered if you died tomorrow unless that represents all you want to be in the future. Give yourself time, hope, and even allow yourself some fantasy and wishful thinking in constructing your story. This exercise requires reflection, silence, being alone with yourself, so take the next 20 minutes to compose a eulogy to your life.*

2. When participants have completed their eulogies, direct them to look around the group and find someone with whom they feel comfortable, whom they like and trust, or who is important to them. (Select the phrase that most appropriately fits the group's level of trust and cohesiveness.) Instruct participants to give their eulogies to that person to be read aloud to the group. Those who receive eulogies of other participants should look over them and be sure they can read them clearly.
3. Each euology should be read aloud carefully, as if the reader were actually responsible to the person for communicating the essence of his or her life.

Variation	Rather than writing a eulogy, participants may wish to construct a collage or other visual eulogy. Magazines, scissors, construction paper, glue, and other art materials are necessary for this variation. Participants will need to explain their collage to their partner for presentation.
Debriefing	1. What was it like to write your eulogy? What did you find easy or difficult? Why? 2. Did you discover anything about yourself or your life? 3. What was it like to read someone else's euology? 4. How was it to hear your own eulogy read? What feelings did this evoke? What thoughts did it trigger? 5. In the process of writing and hearing your eulogy, did you discover any discrepancies between your goals or dreams and the way you live your life now. Do you want to reduce these discrepancies? How might you do this in the immediate future?

---

18. The Clothes We Wear

Goals	1. To assist individuals in identifying important personal values they live by. 2. To assist individuals in exploring their feelings about dying.

The values that we live by are often reflected in the clothing we wear. In this exercise, participants are asked to select three pieces of clothing they would choose to wear at their own funerals. Through this exercise, participants are given the opportunity to identify the values these clothing articles signify to them personally. By asking the participants to select three articles of clothing, they are given the chance to prioritize these values as well as identify them.

Materials	Paper and pencil for each participant.
Time	Approximately 45–60 minutes.
Procedures	1. Ask all participants to imagine that they have only one week left to live. 2. Then ask the participants to imagine the following:

> *During the coming week, you go to your clothes closet and carefully select what you will wear at your own funeral. You pick three different articles of clothing that mean a great deal to you. Each piece of clothing seems to say a lot about you and the way you tried to live. What three pieces do you choose?*

3. Participants write down the articles of clothing and briefly describe the meaning attached to each.

4. Discuss in the whole group or divide into small groups.

Variation

A variation on this activity could include jewelry or a special possession that reflects personal values.

Debriefing

1. What articles of clothing did you select?
2. How did you go about making the decision?
3. What are some of the values reflected by your clothing choice?
4. How much time do you currently spend wearing the kind of clothing you chose? enough or not?
5. What articles of clothing might your loved ones select for you? your parents? your mate? your best friend? Are these clothing selections made by your loved ones for you similar to your own selections? What might this say about how well they currently know you?

---

19. And the Music is You

Goals

1. To identify those musical selections that best represent the continuum of one's life.
2. To reflect, through the medium of music, on those moments that represent significant life experiences.
3. To explore and discuss the role of music in life and death.
4. To examine one's own choice of music for a funeral or memorial service and the function of music in such a service.

Materials

Cassette tape recorder and cassette tapes to do the initial activity. One cassette tape player for each group of two or three at the second session.

Time

This activity needs time between presentation of the assignment and presentation of the individual tapes: 1–1½ hours total.

Procedure

Session 1

Introduce the activity in this way:

Begin by reflecting on the role of music in life from birth through the life span, from the lullabye on. Often a few notes or lyrics can conjure entire emotional experiences for listeners and evoke some of the emotional impact of significant life events.

A funeral or memorial service often includes music and is an opportunity for the survivors to reflect on a life lived and ones still being lived. The music of these services can be personalized.

This exercise is an opportunity to examine your life and to identify, literally, the themes and the melodies of your life.

Think back on your life. Identify pieces of music or songs that represent significant experiences in your life. Select three to five of these and record them on a cassette tape. Bring this tape to the next session.

Session 2

1. Participants divide into groups of two or three with a tape player for each group. The shorter the time for the session, the smaller the group should be. Anticipate 15–20 minutes per person in the group.
2. Each participant plays his or her tape to the subgroup and briefly explains why each selection was made, pointing out the individual significance of this piece of music.
3. Participants discuss why this would or would not be an appropriate tape for their own funeral since it is music that represents significant events in a life from the perspective of the one who has lived that life.
4. Participants may wish to look at any common themes, music, life events, or selections in the small groups.

Variations

1. Have each participant make a tape of songs and music he or she would select for another's funeral or memorial service.
2. Participants might select alternative music from a funeral or memorial service they attended in the past that would reflect their relationship with the person who died and how they viewed that person's life.

Debriefing

1. What process did you go through to identify the music you selected?
2. Were there similar or identical selections in your group? Were there common reasons for these selections? Or were there similar reasons for making very different selections?
3. What range of your life span was covered? Was there any time period that was omitted? Why?
4. What kinds of experiences were linked to the musical selections: individual experiences, relationships, a variety of time periods, happy or easy times, difficult times or events?
5. What significant experiences or types of experiences weren't represented in your selections?
6. What is the role of music at a funeral or memorial service? Who should choose this music? Who typically does choose this music?
7. Would this be an appropriate tape for your funeral or memorial service? Why or why not?
8. Would you share this tape with others in your life? Why or why not?
9. In general, was your music happy or sad tape or an even mix? Does this say anything to you about your own life to this point?
10. Would you change the selections in your tape in any way? Why or why not?

20. Bambi Excerpt

Goals

1. To provide a fairly open-ended tale that has several analogies to the aging process, dying, and loss.
2. To reflect on the ways in which the cycle of life is portrayed in other than human terms, with particular appeal to a child's discussion of death with a parent or other adult.

Materials

Excerpt from *Bambi*, reprinted below.*

Time

20–30 minutes.

Procedures

This excerpt from a literary classic is best given as a reading without interruption and followed by some soliciting of audience response to the story and its meanings, interpretations, and so on. Obviously a rehearsal or two for sense, inflection, timing, and the like is needed, and it may even be helpful to stage the reading a bit by using muted lighting, having participants close their eyes to facilitate picturing the scenario being described.

Briefly, the chapter is a vignette wherein two leaves of advanced age converse about their fates as fall sets in. They review their "lives" and the meaning of their relationship to one another, as well as the effects of aging and concerns over impending "death." It is also worth reading *prior* to telling the audience of its origin or the title of the book.

> *The leaves were falling from the great oak at the meadow's edge. They were falling from all the trees.*
>
> *One branch of the oak reached high above the others and stretched far out over the meadow. Two leaves clung to its very tip.*
>
> *"It isn't the way it used to be," said one leaf to the other.*
>
> *"No," the other leaf answered. "So many of us have fallen off tonight we're almost the only ones left on our branch."*
>
> *"You never know who's going to go next," said the first leaf. "Even when it was warm and the sun shone, a storm or a cloudburst would come sometimes, and many leaves were torn off, though they were still young. You never know who's going to go next."*
>
> *"The sun seldom shines now," sighed the second leaf, "and when it does it gives no warmth. We must have warmth again."*
>
> *"Can it be true," said the first leaf, "can it really be true, that others come to take our places when we're gone and after them still others, and more and more?"*

---

*Felix Salten, *Bambi* (New York: Simon & Schuster, 1956), pp. 72–75. Copyright © 1928, 1956 by Simon & Schuster, Inc. Reprinted by permission of Simon & Schuster, Inc.

"It is really true," whispered the second leaf. *"We can't even begin to imagine it, it's beyond our powers."*

"It makes me very sad," added the first leaf.

They were silent a while. Then the first leaf said quietly to herself, *"Why must we fall? . . ."*

The second leaf asked, *"What happens to us when we have fallen?"*

"We sink down . . ."

"What is under us?"

The first leaf answered, *"I don't know, some say one thing, some another, but nobody knows."*

The second leaf asked, *"Do we feel anything, do we know anything about ourselves when we're down there?"*

The first leaf answered, *"Who knows? Not one of all those down there has ever come back to tell us about it."*

They were silent again. Then the first leaf said tenderly to the other, *"Don't worry so much about it, you're trembling."*

"That's nothing," the second leaf answered, *"I tremble at the least thing now. I don't feel so sure of my hold as I used to."*

"Let's not talk any more about such things," said the first leaf.

The other replied, *"No, we'll let be. But—what else shall we talk about?"* She was silent, but went on after a little while, *"Which of us will go first?"*

"There's still plenty of time to worry about that," the other leaf assured her, *"Let's remember how beautiful it was, how wonderful, when the sun came out and shone so warmly that we thought we'd burst with life. Do your remember? And the morning dew, and the mild and splendid nights . . ."*

"Now the nights are dreadful," the second leaf complained, *"and there is no end to them."*

"We shouldn't complain," said the first leaf gently. *"We've outlived many, many others."*

"Have I changed much?" asked the second leaf shyly but determinedly.

"Not in the least," the first leaf assured her. *"You only think so because I've got to be so yellow and ugly. But it's different in your case."*

"You're fooling me," the second leaf said.

"No, really," the first leaf exclaimed eagerly, *"believe me, you're as lovely as the day you were born. Here and there may be a little yellow spot but it's hardly noticeable and only makes you handsomer, believe me."*

"Thanks," whispered the second leaf, quite touched. *"I don't believe you, not altogether; but I thank you because you're so kind, you've always been so kind to me. I'm just beginning to understand how kind you are."*

"Hush," said the other leaf, and kept silent herself for she was too troubled to talk any more.

Then they were both silent. Hours passed. A moist wind blew, cold and hostile, through the tree-tops. "Ah, now," said the second leaf, "I . . ." Then her voice broke off. She was torn from her place and spun down. Winter had come.

Debriefing

1. Did you like this passage?
2. What did you like? not like?
3. What were the leaves "conversing" about? Why were they talking about it? How did they feel?
4. Have you ever heard anyone else talk like that? Have you ever talked with anyone else like that? If so, how did you feel at the time?
5. How did you feel when the leaf fell?
6. Do you recognize the passage?
7. Can you see using this in any way to help introduce death as a fact of life to a child?

---

21. Me and My Name

Goals

1. To assist participants in developing an increased awareness of the inevitability of death.
2. To provide participants with an opportunity to review, in fantasy, some of the stages of development they have accomplished and some future stages of development they will eventually experience.

Our names are intimately linked with our own personal conception of who we are. By focusing on this one aspect of identity, this exercise gently leads participants into reviewing their life chronology, imagining future events and the inevitability of death.

Setting

Space enough so that participants can stretch out.

Time

Approximately 1 hour.

Procedures

1. Instruct participants to find a comfortable area where they can stretch out, relax, and become aware of themselves.
2. Give brief suggestions for enhancing relaxation and increasing self-awareness: breathing deeply, closing eyes, focusing on body temperature, and so on.
3. Begin a slow-paced structured fantasy during which you describe cues for recollections, past memories, and future projections. Slowly give concrete, vivid memory cues focusing on one particular aspect of the participant's past and future experiences: the participant's name.

It might be good to elaborate on the following examples:

a. The memory of seeing one's name written on a birthday cake, noticing the colors and flavor of the cake. Remembering hearing your name being sung in the "Happy Birthday" song.

b. Seeing in your mind's eye a time when you first printed your name with a crayon or pencil.

c. Remembering seeing your name on a report card, noticing the lettering, seeing the grades given. Hearing your teacher call your name.

d. Seeing in your mind's eye your name written on the collar of a shirt or on gym shorts for identification. Remembering the sound of your name being called by your mother or father.

e. Seeing your name written on a holiday package, noticing the colors and shapes.

f. Remembering hearing your name called to step forward to receive your (high) school diploma; seeing your name written on it.

g. Seeing in your mind's eye your name addressed on the envelope of a love letter. Hearing the sound of your loved one call your name.

h. Imagining seeing in your mind's eye your name written on the cover of *Newsweek*; on a movie marquee; written in the sky with sky writing. Imagining hearing your name repeated on national television.

i. Imagining seeing your name written on an admittance form to a hospital. Hearing the physician pronounce your name.

j. Seeing in your mind's eye your name written on your will.

k. Seeing in your mind's eye your name printed on a death certificate. Hearing your loved ones utter your name as they realize you have died.

l. Seeing your name printed in the obituary column of the newspaper.

m. Seeing your name engraved on a tombstone.

n. Imagining your tombstone five years after your death; 100 years after, 1,000 years after.

4. After allowing several minutes of quiet time, terminate the fantasy by asking participants to open their eyes, stretch, and sit up. Processing the experience might occur in small groups or together as a whole group.

Debriefing

1. What was this experience like for you?

2. Which scenes were you most vividly able to visualize in your mind's eye? Which scenes were harder to visualize?

3. What kind of feelings did you experience in response to seeing your name written in these scenes? in response to hearing your name called in the different scenes?

4. What kind of thoughts did this experience stir up for you about the inevitability of dying?

22. Rocking Chair Fantasy

Goals

1. To assist individuals in identifying attitudes about their past experiences that may be influencing their current feelings about death and dying.
2. To assist individuals in briefly reviewing their lives in order to determine how satisfied they are with their quality and style of living. This exercise may be used as a stimulus for life planning activities.

Acknowledging the inevitability of our own deaths can give us impetus to review the way we have led our lives thus far. Being able to approach an acceptance of the inevitability of our own deaths can also be affected by how satisfied we are with the quality of the life we have led. This exercise is designed to assist individuals in briefly reviewing their lives. Through a guided fantasy experience, participants will be given the opportunity to examine three different "spontaneous memories" from their past. Through individual exploration and group discussion, participants may then be assisted in identifying life-style themes common to each memory and ways these themes may be affecting their attitudes toward dying.

Materials

A quiet, comfortable environment with comfortable chairs.

Time

Approximately 1 hour.

Procedure

Begin by asking the participants if they would be willing to participate in a guided fantasy experience. If participants are willing, instruct them to find a comfortable place in the room to go to, sit down, and take a few minutes to relax. Suggest that they concentrate on their breathing during these few minutes in order to assist them in relaxing. Then give the following general verbal instructions:

I would like you to close your eyes and imagine that you have only one year left to live. You firmly believe that the medical evidence is accurate. Now that you know you will soon die, you decide to sit quietly and review your life. You find an old comfortable rocking chair on a porch or in a room that is peaceful and quiet, and you sit and gently rock. You sit rocking, back and forth, back and forth, back and forth. And as you rock gently back and forth, you remember three different experiences in your life. Each memory comes to you spontaneously, events from your past that you can see so clearly in your mind's eye in detail. With each memory in turn you notice the vivid details.

Your turn your attention to the first memory and you look very carefully. You notice what you are doing, you see the expres-

sion on your face, you notice whether other people are in the memory, and if so you notice the expression on their faces and you remember how you felt. (pause) You now turn your attention to the second memory and again you notice what you are doing, you see the expression on your face, you notice whether other people are there and if so you see their faces, and you can feel how you felt. (pause) Now focus on a third and final distinct memory: noticing your behavior and that of any others involved. (pause) And as you sit in your rocking chair, rocking back and forth, back and forth, you reflect on your three memories. As you reflect, you notice whether the expression in your face in each memory was the same or different. You notice whether you were smiling or laughing or quiet or sad looking. You also reflect on the other people in your memories, and you notice if the same people were in each. And as you sit and rock back and forth and reflect on what you were doing in each memory, and the expression on your face, you see what these memories might show about the way you led your life. And you ask yourself whether you are satisfied with these three particular memories as accurately reflecting the best qualities of your life. (pause) As you see what these memories showed, you notice the expression on your face as you continue to rock back and forth, and you notice how you feel.

Then instruct the participants to continue to imagine rocking and reflecting for a few minutes and to return gently to the present moment as you count slowly from one to ten.

Debriefing

1. What was this experience like for you?
2. How clearly were you able to see your memories?
3. What kinds of expressions did you see on your face in each memory? Were you surprised at what you saw?
4. Who were the other people in your memories? What kinds of expressions did you see on their faces? What might this show about the way they felt for you then and now? What might this say about the way you feel about them now?
5. What was happening in your memories? How did you feel about how each memory turned out—pleased? satisfied? embarrassed? hurt? disappointed?
6. Did each memory turn out about the same or different?
7. After you had reviewed all three memories and you were rocking in your rocking chair, what kind of expression did you see on your face then? How satisfied are you now with these three memories as accurately reflecting the best qualities of your life so far?
8. How might your memories be related to how accepting you now are toward the inevitability of the deaths of those you love? toward your own death?

23. The Pecking Order of Death

Goals
1. To provide a guided fantasy experience in anticipating loss.
2. To assist participants to take stock of the significant others in their life space.
3. To enable people to gain a perspective on the meanings of death occurring both in and out of turn.

This is an exercise in self-exploration designed to give participants a different view of whom they value and how they prize those relationships in the light of their death or other loss. It can assist the learner in defining anew the importance placed on renewal and recognition of those living persons and the potential effects of their death—as well as one's own—in time.*

Setting
Preferably a closed room where light can be dimmed or shut out; one free from other distracting noise and intrusions and one having comfortable seats.

Time
Approximately 30–40 minutes (expandable).

Procedures
Introduce the coming experience as a guided fantasy, a brief experiment in exploring one's so-called place in life (in death). Indicate to participants that it will help to dim the lights, have their eyes gently closed, and get comfortable in their seats. Then direct them through the following series of thoughts. (It is best to rehearse this with an audiotape or other person before doing it with a large group, particularly so timing and pauses and inflection can be mastered to elicit a satisfactory imagery experience):

> *Relax for a moment. When your mind is quiet and without pressure, let a neutral visual field form itself in your mind's eye. When this background field has established itself, visualize the face of somebody you care about, a person who is important to you. See this person's face as though it were a suddenly illuminated light bulb glowing against the nondescript background. Keep this face in view. But now think of somebody else you care about. Watch how this face appears and lights up in your mind's eye as well. You now have the inner presence of two people who are important to you. Now visualize a third person you care about, in the same way as you have visualized the others, who are still present . . . now a fourth person . . . a fifth person . . .*

---

*This activity is the creation of Robert Kastenbaum. It first appeared in N. Datan and L. Ginsberg, eds., *Life-span developmental psychology: Normative crises and interventions*. (New York: Academic Press, 1976). Reprinted with permission.

a sixth person . . . a seventh person. That will do. Your mind now contains visually, explicitly the symbols of seven important people.

One of these people will die before the others. You do not know for sure who this will be, but you do have a guess or feeling about it. Extinguish that person's face. The light goes out where that face had been; the other lights are still on. Time goes by. Another person dies. Watch this person's light go out. The other lights are on, but now there are two dark spots. More time elapses. Another person dies; another light goes out. Three people gone; four remaining. Which light will be the next to be extinguished? Time goes by, and a fourth light goes out. Only three of your important people remain illuminated in your mind's eye. Now another dies. Which of the remaining two will be the next to die, which the survivor? More time elapses. And another light goes out. Your mind's eye, only a few moments ago populated by some of the people closest and most significant to you, now is dark except for a single face.

Halt the thought experiment here, but keep your eyes closed and reflect upon the following questions:

The survivor in your mind's eye—is this perhaps the youngest of the important people you visualized at the outset?

The first person to die—was it perhaps the oldest of the important people you visualized at the outset?

As individuals continued to die, did you continue to respond implicitly to each death in its full particularity—or, at a certain point, did the mass of accumulated loss take precedence over specific bereavement?

In what ways did your thoughts and feelings fluctuate between concern for those who were gone and those who were remaining? Did you find your mind and your heart divided between the living and the dead?

One final question, if you will: Where does your own face, your own life and fate, belong in this sequence? Would you have been the first to perish? The last? Who of these people do you implicitly expect to survive? Who will survive you?

Now I'm going to raise the lights again and ask you to open your eyes slowly and return your thoughts to here and now, where we'll see what kinds of experiences our little thought experiment provided.

Debriefing

Either in small subgroups or with the entire group, some further inquiry along the following lines is needed to gain some reflected closure on the experience.

1. What was the experience like for you? How are you feeling about it now?
2. What were your answers to the questions posed regarding youngest to die, oldest to die, and your probable place in the sequence?
3. Did the "most important" or "closest" one predecease you, or would you die first? What are the implications of that for you? for them?
4. Did you feel resistant or unable to envision anyone who came to mind? Why was that? Did it feel real at all?
5. Does this type of experience concern you as tampering with fate or magical thinking in any way?
6. At some point, did you notice yourself feeling numbed at the accumulated loss you sensed.
7. Does this experience say anything to you about your own sense of cherishing your relationships with these people and how you demonstrate that or renew its vitality?

---

24. Planning the Last Day

Goals

1. To heighten awareness of the inevitability of death and sensitivity to issues relating to interpersonal loss.
2. To promote discussion and insight relating to interpersonal attachments, change, loss, and grief.

All too often, most of us take for granted the people we care most about. With our busy schedules, it can be easy to create the illusion that we have plenty of time to spend with the people we love—tomorrow or the next day. This exercise is designed to promote discussion about the finiteness of life and to assist participants in developing an increased awareness about the quality of their interpersonal living.

Materials

Paper and pencils for each participant.

Time

Approximately 1 hour.

Procedure

1. Distribute paper and pencils to each participant and instruct them each to find a place in the room where they can reflect comfortably alone.
2. After each participant has secured a comfortable position, give the following general instructions:

   Close your eyes and take a few minutes to deeply relax. [Offer relaxation suggestions here.] *Now think of some person you know very well and care very much for* (pause) *When you have thought of such a person, please indicate by raising your index finger. [After each participant has raised an index finger, continue.]*

Imagine that this person will soon have to leave you forever. Before she or he goes, that person asks you to plan an entire day especially for him or her. You are asked to plan the whole day in a way that would make the person very happy. You feel very special that you have such a chance, and you begin to plan that day. Think about how you would plan the day and then open your eyes and write down your answers to the following questions:

1. On the day, what time would you arrange for your special person to wake up? How would you wake that person up? (pause)

2. What would your special person like for breakfast? Where would he or she want to eat it? (pause)

3. What clothes would you pick for your special person to wear? (pause)

4. What would you arrange to do in the morning? (pause)

5. What would your special person like for lunch? Where? (pause)

6. What kind of activities would you plan for the afternoon? with whom? (pause)

7. What would your special person like for dinner? Where? (pause)

8. What would you plan for evening activities? (pause)

9. How would you say good-bye at the end of your time together?

Note to the leader: Because of the emotional intensity of the last question, you might want to talk about experiencing feelings.

3. After an appropriate pause for reflection, utilize either or both of the following discussion strategies:

    1. Request that participants form dyads, triads, or small groups to discuss the days they planned and process the experience.

    2. Discuss the exercises with the entire group.

Debriefing

1. What was this experience like for you?

2. What was it like for you to try to design a day for someone you care about? What kind of activities did you plan?

3. What feelings did you have about spending the last day with your special person?

4. How did these feelings affect the way you planned the day? How might these feelings affect the way you might actually spend that last day?

5. How does this exercise and discussion leave you feeling about your special person?

25. Saying the Last Goodbye

Goals

1. To assist participants in gaining deeper levels of awareness about one aspect of the dying process: leaving loved ones.
2. To provide a structure whereby participants can explore their own current feelings of love and caring for the special people in their lives.

Whether it is dealt with directly or indirectly, dying involves saying goodbye to the people we love. While we can think about saying goodbye, it gives us an abstract awareness of how we might actually feel to leave those people we care most about. A much deeper level of awareness can be reached by verbalizing our goodbyes as we search for the words, voice tone, and tempo that would capture the depth of feeling associated with that experience.

Setting

A quiet, safe environment where participants can feel free to explore and discuss their thoughts and emotional reactions openly.

Time

Approximately 2 hours

Procedures

This exercise may stir up fairly intense emotional reactions for some participants. You might take time to talk about experiencing and expressing feelings. You need also to allow sufficient time at the end of the exercise for adequate debriefing and discussion. Mention that members can opt out of the exercise if they wish.

1. Ask participants to pair up. The dyads then find a place in the room where they each can converse comfortably without undue interference from others.
2. Participants close their eyes and imagine which five people they would want most to say goodbye to if they knew they would soon be taking a trip that would take them away for a lifetime.
3. Each participant then writes down the names of each of the five people.
4. Give the following general instructions to the group:

   Spend a few minutes thinking about the first person on your list. See if you can make a very vivid picture of this person's face in your mind's eye. Allow yourself to remember in rich detail some of the different experiences you've shared with this person. As you remember different experiences, pick one in particular that stands out in your memory. Take a close look at this memory. As you look closely, ask yourself: "What have I learned about living from this person?" Take a few minutes to ponder this question and then write down your answer. Then proceed to the next person on your list and go through the same steps until you have a statement of what you've learned about living from each of the five persons on your list.

5. After each participant has completed this, give the following general instructions to each of the dyads:

   Sit directly across from your partner. Take the first person on your list and imagine your partner is that person. Describe to your partner, as if you were talking directly to the person on your list, the particular experience you recalled. Describe this experience as vividly as you can. Take time to describe what makes the experience important to you. As a closing farewell, verbalize with tone of voice and tempo that is congruent with your feelings: "As a reminder of the special times we've shared together, I leave you with this lesson of living I've learned from you [Describe what your have learned.] Thank you. Goodbye."

6. Ask the participants to pause and reflect on the feelings that emerge from this experience.
7. Instruct partners in the dyads to switch roles and follow the same steps until each member of the dyad has described experiences and lessons about life for each of the people on their list.

At the conclusion of the exercise, ask the entire group of participants to form a close circle to debrief the experience.

Debriefing

1. What was this experience like for you?
2. What kind of feelings were stirred up for you by this experience?
3. What were some of the lessons of life that you have learned from the special people in your lives?
4. What was it like for you to verbalize what you have learned and to thank them? to say goodbye?
5. How do you now feel about the five people on your list?
6. What other reactions did you have to this experience?

4 Role Plays

This set of SLEs is a collection of role-playing opportunities. They are simultaneously the most difficult and potentially the most enriching to carry out. When used effectively, they can be the most poignant and even profound learning experiences with which one can teach. But they also are the most demanding on all concerned. By all means, some experimenting with combinations of these and with role-play coaching of participants are encouraged.

We have added a second level of scenarios with related roles for enactment. These are really a next level in terms of complexity and demand. They pose truly knotty questions and illuminate dilemmas that have come to the fore only very recently. All are based on actual occurrences. They pose more difficult psychosocial and bioethical quandaries than the initial group of role plays, calling for thoughtful reflection made all the more troubling by the lack of absolutes guiding satisfactory resolution. We urge facilitators to warm up to them by trying some of the lower-level-demand role plays first.

1. The Mayflower

Goals

To provide an emotional context and insight into a historical event or series of events with moribund features.

Setting

Room with a large open space.

Materials

Facilitator may want to be familiar with several accounts of Pilgrim and Puritan history and the journey of the *Mayflower*, as well as diary accounts of the first year in the New World.

Procedures

All participants (save one member to be held out at beginning) assemble at one corner of the room. When all are gathered standing, begin to provide the group with its identity and circumstances:

> We are going to do some group role playing of a significant historical event. As I narrate the scenario, imagine yourself as a real member of this actual group. See if you can "get into" it. Let's begin.
>
> It is 1608, and you are in England. Due to religious differences with the government, you relocate to live in Holland. Most of you are craftspeople for whom work and social integration in the new home are not easily found.
>
> You weather those trials for over ten years, until you grow weary of the difficulties of such a life-style, and, fearing that your children will lose all touch with their cultural heritage, you decide to go to the New World. There you hope to find better opportunities to preserve your culture and community, as well as less restriction on the expression of your religious values.
>
> So, on August 5, 1620, you have returned to Southhampton, England, and are embarking on such a journey aboard a pair of former wine carrying vessels, the *Mayflower* and the *Speedwell.* [Begin to move the group slowly toward the opposite side of the room.]
>
> You're not even at sea for two weeks when the *Speedwell* begins to leak, and thus both ships return to England. [Move the group back to its original place.]
>
> Since the leak turns out not to be repairable, 102 people—73 men and 29 women and children—crowd onto the *Mayflower* and set sail again in early September. [Instruct the group to crowd very closely together.]
>
> Only 35 of the total are Pilgrims! Twenty-five are the ship's crew, and the rest are people being sent by an English company to start a new colony. The crossing is arduous! [Begin moving the group slowly across the room.] Many are sick! [Stop the group and have them rock back and forth while holding their stomachs and foreheads.] One man dies! [Arbitrarily pick one male out of the group and retire him from the group.] A short while later, a child named Oceanus is born. [Have the withheld person crowd into the group and have the group move over to the opposite wall and then back them up five steps, then forward—repeating this three times.]
>
> Finally, after sixty-six days at sea, and after nearly another month wandering the coastline to find a suitable landing and settlement, it is December 26, 1620, and you are in the midst of winter in a foreign unsettled place. As you begin to erect home sites, the long journey, weather, and lack of agricultural know-

how combine to take their toll of healthy settlers. You expected to live by fishing and fur trading but have no usable equipment. You know nothing of ice fishing, trapping and trading here, and you have no farming experience. Your heritage is not farming but crafts. In the first two months your collective "catch" is one cod, three seals, and an eagle. You're exceedingly cold, hungry, and lonely. Sickness strikes and, within three months, half of you die, often at a rate of two or three each day. [At this point, either by pointing out or tapping half the members, "kill" 50 percent who are to leave the group and take seats.]

Only 50 people of the original 102 are left. Not only do many die, but most of the living are too sick to work or even get around. [At this point, tap all but one-seventh—calculate in advance—of the group, instructing those picked out to sit or squat down where they are.]

You who are well must bury the dead, care for the sick, and try to stay well and survive yourselves. In March, things begin to look up, as your leader, Miles Standish, helps you befriend two native Americans, Samoset and Squanto, who speak some English. Squanto introduces you to Massasoit, the chief of the Wampanoags. You make several accords, and in the spring of 1621 the Indians teach you how to survive by being farmers. They show you, for instance, how to plant corn using fish for soil fertilizer, and your first crop comes in beautifully in midsummer. [Have the standees pull the "sick" up to indicate a gradual return to health.]

By autumn, your situation looks much better, and you decide to celebrate by holding a feast called "Harvest Home." It is based on celebrations you held in England. Governor Bradford, your elected leader, invites the Wampanoags to the feast, which goes on for three days. The Indians bring food along to share, and the menu consists of turkey, venison, duck, clams, corn, squash, wild fruits and berries, cornbread, ale, wine, and many other good foods.

This first Thanksgiving was a playful time, with wrestling matches, marching drills, foot races, lacrosse, and other games played by all.

In early 1622, another ship arrives, but when it returns to England, none of you sail on it! As the years went by, the idea of a Thanksgiving Day was taken up by some of the other colonies. In November 1789, George Washington issued the first presidential message saying we should have a day of thanks and commemoration. In 1863, President Abraham Lincoln proclaimed that a national Thanksgiving Day should be on a fixed Thursday in November. And today we know what that feast has come to be. Thus ends our historical trip.

Debriefing
1. What things bound you together as a community?
2. How was your trip?
3. What was your feeling when the first person in your group died? when the child was born?
4. What were your feelings when you finally made it to the new land? when you found out what it was like?
5. How did you feel when so many people began to die? if you were one who stayed alive? if you were one who died?
6. How did you feel if you were a sick survivor? a well one?
7. What was your feeling in spring?
8. What feelings did you have for the community?
9. Was it worth it?
10. Why didn't anyone go back?

2. Answering Children's Questions about Death

Goals
1. To give participants practice in responding to typical queries children address to adults and older siblings about death and dying.
2. To gain some understanding for the developmental complexity of various ways of responding to different levels of understanding.
3. To get feedback on the *appropriateness*, *accuracy*, and *comfort* with which one responds to children's questions.

Setting
A room large enough for a single seat amid a circle of seats adequate for the number of participants, with a recommended maximum of eight to ten per group.

Materials
A set of cards (3 × 5 inch or smaller) with the following ages and questions on them in equal numbers to the total of the group. Examples follow:

> 5 year old: "Where is 'dead'?"
> 6 year old: "Will I die when I am old too?"
> 7 year old: "Will I ever see Grandpa again?" (question asked after burial of grandfather)
> 7 year old: "Don't people die when they go to the hospital?"
> 4 year old: "It's only 'bad guys' who get killed. Right?"
> 13 year old: "I'll never get over her death, will you?" (speaking of a peer's death)
> 8 year old: "Was Mommy angry with me? She didn't say good-bye when she died."
> 9 year old: "What happens when a person is burned up?" (cremated)
> 6 year old: "Can you tell me what happens when a person dies? Do they go to heaven or hell or what?"
> 15 year old: "Why didn't Dad want to go on living?"

Time	5 minutes per group member plus 20 minutes to debrief.
Procedures	1. The group is gathered in a circle with a chair in the center for each "child" to be portrayed.
	2. Each participant is given a card in turn that has the question he or she is to ask and elaborate on briefly and a notation of the age of the questioner.
	3. Randomly, each group member selects one of the outer circle members to be the respondent. (The leader may stipulate that no one person be called on more than once or twice.)
	4. The question and role-play exchange should not exceed 3 minutes each, with the respondent becoming the next role player.
	5. At the end of each question-and-answer segment, the remainder of the group is to comment in critique on the respondent's answer along the dimensions of appropriateness (developmentally), accuracy (validity of response), and comfort (exhibited while responding; verbal and nonverbal).
	6. After the entire group has had a turn at each role once, the group facilitator leads some summary discussion of the impact of such an exercise.
Debriefing	1. How did the experience of being asked these questions by a "young person" strike you?
	2. Which role was easier? Why?
	3. Did you draw on past experiences either in asking or answering questions after you began the role play?
	4. Did you give specific identity to others when answering the question?
	5. Did your anxiety level increase or decrease after the initial exchange as the role play developed?
	6. What developmental differences did you notice? How did answers change depending on developmental level? How did questioning change?
	7. Was your role as answerer affected by your role as questioner?
	8. What other questions would you think appropriate?
	9. Are these also questions that might be asked by adults?
	10. Did this exercise help you? Why or why not?

3. Potlatch

Goals	To design and experience a potlatch and its life and death values. Participants will examine individual and group values, symbols, and attitudes toward death and the cultural and communal aspects of rituals related to death and dying.
Materials	*Session 1:* Dictionary, paper, pencil, books that define a potlatch.

Session 2: Paper, pencils, and pens.
Session 3: Any materials identified in the second session.

Time

Three 40-minute sessions.

Procedures

Session 1

This session is divided into three segments. The first 15–20 minutes should be devoted to individual research. Participants will use a variety of materials to gather information on a potlatch and take notes. This can also be done prior to the session, with notes brought by each participant. In the second segment (15 minutes), participants will share findings and, third, break into groups of eight to twelve, which will work together in the next session.

For the session it is important to have a variety of materials available so that each participant may do research using several resources. Although there may be duplicated material, a variety of both descriptions and definitions is important. This activity may be done in relation to any study of culture, social studies or any course that covers ritual, custom, symbols or values.

Session 2

Participants work in their groups for the purpose of designing a potlatch. To do this the group members will need to identify attitudes, symbols, roles, and rituals and their significance. By the end of this session, each person in the group should have an identified role in the potlatch presentation, and the group should have identified a list of materials needed for the presentation and know who will provide them.

Session 3

It is often best to have this session after a lapse of several days to allow group members to do additional planning and also allow each individual to examine his or her role in the potlatch. At this session, each small group will present a potlatch for the entire group and answer any questions about their presentation. Also they will discuss the exercise.

Variations

A potlatch is native to the culture of Indian tribes of the Northwest Pacific. A variation of this activity could focus on other cultural or ethnic rituals and celebrations used in connection with death, dying, or the dead. Many of these rituals reflect cultural beliefs, attitudes, and expressions related to both life and death. They allow participants to explore the ways of culture views both the separations from and the connections between the living and the dead.

Debriefing

1. Do you like the custom of the potlatch?
2. What were the characteristics of the culture you portrayed?

3. What attitudes toward death were expressed?
4. What attitudes toward life were expressed?
5. What, if any, similar rituals exist in your culture or background?
6. How did your understanding of a potlatch differ from the first session to the third?

---

4. Suicide Myths

Goals

1. To examine and dispute commonly held beliefs about suicide.
2. To conduct open dialogue about personal and social attitudes toward suicidal behavior.

Materials

A series of cards or papers with one of the following myths stated on each (plus a summary list for viewing or distribution):

1. Suicidal people always give cues in advance of making a life-threatening gesture, such as by withdrawing socially, giving away personal items, or abusing alcohol.
2. People who kill themselves rarely do so in the initial attempt.
3. Only when the depression in a suicidal person seems to lift can others feel the crisis has passed.
4. Suicidal people are so almost chronically, seeming constantly on the verge of another gesture to end their lives.
5. Most suicidal gestures are not serious but are merely help-seeking cries for rescue.
6. Suicidal tendencies are inherited.
7. Getting a suicidal person to talk about his or her despair is an excellent way to prevent him or her from acting self-destructively.
8. The root cause of a person's suicide can be found if the crises that result from his or her life circumstances are scrutinized.
9. Suicide is a sign of insanity.
10. Suicide is a cowardly act.

Participants should sit in a circle, with the leader deciding how many myths, and therefore how many persons, per grouping.

Time

50 minutes.

Procedures

1. Introduce the exercise by saying, ''We are going to have a short lesson in small groups that deals with a number of widely held beliefs about suicide in this society today. Some of them may be mythical rather than true statements.''
2. Distribute cards or sheets with a statement printed on each (prepared in advance), one to each member of the group. Participants read the myth quietly to themselves and await the next instruction. If they are unsure of the meaning of the statement they received, they should privately seek clarification from the leader.

3. In turn, each member will:
   a. Read the statement aloud.
   b. Indicate whether he or she believes it is valid.
   c. Solicit agreement by a show of hands in the group.
   d. Ask any or all minority opinions to tell why they disagree with others.
   e. State why she or he chose the position.
   f. Invite open group dialogue about the statement (5 minutes).
   After calling time at 5 minutes, the leader restates the myth and gives a brief commentary on why the statement is invalid currently. He or she can also elaborate on the consequences, history, and possible methods for countering the myth, asking volunteers for their input in summary and for any specific (to the myth) questions.

4. The process is repeated for the rest of each group's membership until all have shared their myths. Obviously, any disclosure of the fact that all the statements are invalid will detract from the experience, so that should not be divulged in conducting the activity. Five minutes per group member is sufficient for the round.

5. After the round has been completed, each group should select a spokesperson and proceed to debrief the activity. Allow 15–20 minutes more for debriefing, and then solicit short summary statements from each spokesperson for another 10 minutes. Finish by distributing or displaying the collection of myths used.

Variations

The full set of myths can also be given as a sort of true-false listing. Then have participants debate their reasons for holding different positions along the same lines of discussion as above. Following debriefing, provide a key to the myths and make a brief lecture out of that set of explanations. Polling the total group at the conclusion of each statement if read aloud at the end, and possibly tallying the agreement for the total group, are variants to dealing with the information that can add significant demonstrations of social or group positions.

Debriefing

1. What basic motive(s) might underlie the support given to certain beliefs about suicidal behavior?
2. Were there any apparent sex, age, or other patterns of differences in beliefs held by your subgroup (or the whole membership, if polled)?
3. What particular myth(s) received the most support as valid? Which the least? What surprises emerged for you? Why?
4. Was there any felt or apparent wavering on any statement as a result of group pressure?
5. How might the knowledge gained here about mythologies about suicide affect your behaviors and attitudes?

4.1 Level 1 Role-Playing Scenarios Relating to Death, Loss, and Separation

Goals

1. To assist participants in gaining insight into how they might feel and respond to a situation associated with death and loss.
2. To assist participants in recognizing that there are wide variations in feelings, responses, and interactions for each situation.

Role-playing exercises provide the opportunity to examine feelings, attitudes, and thoughts about a situation prior to having to deal with the situation. Participants have a chance to gain an experiential understanding, explore options, and examine responses to potentially difficult situations within a structure that provides opportunity for discussion and insight. Role-playing exercises are particularly useful in assisting participants in gaining more than just an intellectual understanding by integrating the cognitive and affective dimensions of the learning exercise. Consequently these exercises can be particularly effective teaching tools for instruction in the area of death and loss.

Materials

Instruction sheets describing the individual roles to be played; Information sheet listing constructive guidelines for role playing' name tags and markers.

Time

1–2 hours.

Procedures

Because role-play situations are enacted in the first person and have a here-and-now focus, the level of emotional involvement for the participants can become quite intense. Ensure that participation is voluntary and that participants can feel free to end the role-playing exercises at any time.

1. Give a rationale for the value of role playing exercises. Then distribute "Tips for Role Playing" to participants and discuss these prior to beginning the role plays.

2. Participants who volunteer to play the roles are given an envelope or index card that contains a description of their role to be played. Role players also receive name tags. For each situation, the role players are asked to leave the room briefly to study their respective parts. They are asked not to converse with each other until the exercise begins. Each role player receives instructions that might read as follows: "As you read your role description, take a few minutes to think about how you might feel if you were actually that person. Reflect silently without talking to others. On your name tag, write a new name for yourself for your role and wear the name tag during your role play. As soon as you have a good idea for your role, return to the room to begin."

3. While the role players are studying their parts, a description of the role-playing situation can be given to the rest of the participants. These people can be invited to imagine how they might engage in their own portrayal of the parts.

4. When the role players are ready, they return to the room and are asked to enact the situation. Allow the role plays to continue as long as productive interactions are taking place but not more than 10–15 minutes each, depending on total time allocated.

5. At the conclusion of the role play, remind the role players that it is useful to stay in role when initially discussing their feelings and responses to the role play.

Debriefing

Some Questions for the Role Players

1. How do you feel in the role of _____?
2. What feelings do you have about the persons you've been interacting with?
3. What do you think they feel about you?

After assisting the role players in discussing their reactions, instruct the role players to step out of role and join the rest of the students in a discussion of the role-play exercise:

Some Questions for the Class Members

1. What were you feeling during the role-playing exercise?
2. How might you have responded differently if you were in this situation? What other ways of responding can you think of?
3. If this situation were to occur in real life, what might the individuals need to handle the situation constructively?

Tips for Role Playing

Suggestions to Role Players

Role-playing exercises are structured to give you the opportunity to act temporarily like another person. Through role playing you are given the chance to step into another person's shoes and see the world from that person's perspective. You will be able to learn more from the experience if you wholeheartedly try to become that person as completely as you can. Here are some suggestions that you might follow:

1. Spend a few minutes thinking about the person whose role you are playing. Ask yourself: "How would I feel if I really were this person? How would I behave? How would I try to express myself?
2. During the role-play exercise, respond as spontaneously as you can.
3. You will be more effective as a role player if you are able to concentrate your attention just on the role players involved in your situation. Try to ignore the rest of the group.
4. Try to give your role play your best effort. Clowning around is not helpful.

Suggestions for Observers

You can assist the role players by remaining silent during the role plays. Try to identify with one of the role players and feel what he or she might be feeling. Rather than judge the quality of the acting, try to imagine how you might respond if you were engaged in that role play.

Level 1 Scenarios

Situation 1: Parent and Child

Parent: Your 8-year-old child's pet dog, Muffy, has just been hit by an automobile and killed. Your child is arriving home from school and doesn't yet know that the dog has been killed.

Child: You are just arriving home from school. You are 8 years old and are excited about going outside to play when you get home. You are also excited about telling your parents about how well you did in school today. As you walk through the door you notice that your dog, Muffy, is not around as he usually is. You call his name and ask where he is.

Situation 2: College Roommates

Roommate A: Your roommate is in class. You have just received a call from her father. He was very distraught and was trying to reach your roommate to tell her to come home immediately. He told you that her mother, who had been very ill, just died. He hangs up without specifically telling you whether you should be the one to tell your roommate that her mother is dead.

Roommate B: You are returning from biology class to your room at college. You expect to see your roommate and to continue talking about your big date for the coming weekend. You are excited because this will be the first weekend in over a month that you will be at school. The last several weekends you have driven the 200 miles home to be with your mother who has been sick in the hospital. You are worried about her but have been assured by your mother and rest of your family that they'll call you if there's anything you can do.

Situation 3:   Family Investment

Physician: You have recently completed diagnostic tests on a 20-year-old woman. Cancer has been discovered in the lower thigh of her right leg, and it is necessary that her leg be amputated immediately in order to decrease the chances of cancer spreading. However, you known that there is a very strong chance that the cancer may have already spread, leaving your patient in danger for her life. Your patient is an outstanding ballet dancer who is currently dancing for the university dance troupe. Her lifelong aspiration has been to become a professional dancer.

Patient: You are a 20-year-old woman who is recognized as an outstanding ballet dancer. Currently you are dancing for the university dance troupe. You have always dreamed of becoming a professional ballet dancer. Four weeks ago you began to experience pain in your right leg. You assume that the pain in your leg is due to the strains from long hours of practice and are anxious to have it remedied so you can return to your full practice schedule.

Parent: You are the mother of a 20-year-old woman. You are accompanying your daughter to the physician to learn the results of her diagnostic tests. Your daughter is an outstanding ballet dancer. You are very proud of your daughter's success, and you enthusiastically share her dream that she become a professional ballet dancer. Four weeks ago your daughter began experiencing pain in her right leg. At first you were not concerned. But now you are very worried about the potential seriousness of your daughter's ailment. You feel compelled to find out everything you can from the physician about the diagnosis. You demand the physician give you concrete answers about the ailment, treatment, and the prognosis. You keep pushing until you feel you have all the facts.

Situation 4:   Religious Issues

Friend A: You best friend's father has been diagnosed with terminal cancer and is expected to die in a matter of weeks. You know that religious faith is very important to your friend, and he firmly believes that his religious faith will somehow protect his father from dying.

Friend B: Your father has been diagnosed with terminal cancer. The physicians have told you and your family that your father is expected to die in just a matter of weeks. You have a deep conviction in your religious faith and firmly believe your faith will somehow protect your father from dying. You are with your best friend, and you are curious about his religious views and ask him. Does he also believe in the power of your faith to protect your father from dying?

Situation 5: Attitudes of Helpers toward Death

Physician (or other helper): Your patient has widespread cancer of the lung, and it is anticipated she will die in a matter of weeks.

Patient: You know you have cancer of the lung. You are very frightened and ask, "Am I going to die?" After hearing the answer, you ask, "What will death be like? What would you feel, doctor, if you were me?"

Situation 6: Communication about Loss

Nurse: Your patient is a 29-year-old woman who is a very outgoing, energetic, vibrant person. You know that yesterday she was informed by the physician that her right breast would have to be surgically removed due to cancer. However, you also know that the patient was not informed about the full implications of her diagnosis. There seems to be clear indication that the cancer may have spread. The prognosis for her is actually poor, with the likelihood that she may die soon. You are visiting the patient to prepare her for surgery the following day. You know that your patient thinks that she will recover quickly after the operation. You wonder whether you should tell her the whole truth or instead try to keep the patient's spirit up.

Patient: You are a 29-year-old woman who has always been highly energetic and outgoing. Several weeks ago, you discovered a lump in your breast. Yesterday you were informed by your physician that your right breast must be removed immediately. Surgery is scheduled for tomorrow. You are in the hospital. A nurse whom you feel comfortable with has just come in to see you. There are so many questions you would like to have answered, especially from another woman. Since you and your fiancee are planning to be married in three months, you ask the nurse whether she thinks he will still find you sexually appealing. Other questions: Will you be able to go swimming next summer? If so, what kind of bathing suit should you wear? Will you be able to play tennis? go skiing? You ask the nurse how she might feel if she herself would have to lose her breast. You also ask the nurse what the risks of the operation really are.

Situation 7: Guilt

Friend A: Your friend's older brother was recently killed in an automobile accident. Since the accident, your friend has talked incessantly about how guilty he feels. He states over and over again, "It should have been me that was killed, not my brother, Jim." You care for your friend, a very great deal, and try to comfort him as best you can.

Friend B: Several weeks ago your older brother, Jim, was killed in an automobile accident. Since the accident, you have been terribly distraught. Down deep inside you feel extremely guilty. On the day of the accident, you and Jim had an argument over who was to get to use the car. He won the argument and took the car. At the time you were so angry you secrectly wished he would "drop dead." Now you feel so guilty that you wish it was you who died and not Jim. You are visiting with a good friend, and you find yourself saying, "It should have been me that was killed."

Situation 8: "Right to Die"

Roommate A: You have recently returned to school after having visited your parents over the weekend. During your visit you had a serious discussion with your father about death and illness. Your father made a request: Should he ever be bedridden with a terminal disease, he wants you to make sure that no efforts are made to prolong his life through medication or any other means. He prefers to let the disease run its course and to die naturally. You told your father that you would need to think about his request before giving him an answer.

When you returned to school, you decided to talk to your roommate about this issue. You explain your situation to your roommate and then ask her what she might do if she were you. After you listen to her response, you try to explain how you feel.

Roommate B: Your roommate has recently returned after having visited with her parents. You can sense that something has been on her mind since the visit, and you imagine that she might like to talk to you about it. You do your best to be available to her.

Situation 9: Loss

Friend A: Your best friend recently broke his leg on a skiing trip. He will be in a cast for several months. Prior to breaking his leg, he was an outstanding athlete who actively competed in basketball, baseball, and soccer. Since breaking his leg, he has seemed withdrawn and hard to talk to. You wonder what is going on with him and ask him.

Friend B: Recently you broke your leg on a skiing trip and will be in a cast for several months. The physicians have hinted that you might not regain full use of your leg because it was a serious break. Prior to your accident, you were an outstanding athlete who competed in basketball, baseball, and soccer. Often you even dream of becoming a professional athlete. Now, although you've never told anyone, you are afraid you might never be able to run again. Lately you've been spending more and more time alone because it's hard for you to see your friends being active and having fun. Sometimes you just want to scream out how unfair it is. Sometimes it makes you furious to see how much your friends take their health for granted, and you find yourself secretly asking, "Why me and not them?" One of your best friends has just dropped by to see you. Suddenly during your conversation, you blurt out how frustrated and angry you are.

4.2 Level 2 Role-Playing Scenarios Relating to Death, Loss, and Separation

Situation 1: Family and Hospice

Husband/Father: You are a 79-year-old male whose prostate cancer has metastasized two years after your initial treatment. You have lost all feeling in your legs and are confined to bed. Other than that, you feel pretty good physically. Your doctor told you that there is no further treatment he can offer and that you will not be cured. You have elected to go home until you die. Your son, who lives 700 miles away, suggested hospice care and even came when you got out of the hospital the last time. He was there when your hospice care started and when all the strangers started to come into your home.

Your wife and daughter, who lives within walking distance and visits daily, became increasingly distressed by all the strangers, the hospice people, coming into your home all the time. They have gradually been able to tell them to stay away so that now only the nurse is let in about once a week. Your wife and daughter seem to be angry all the time. They yell at you for bringing these strangers in, blame you for being sick, say you must not really be dying but just pretending, and seem to be mad all the time. You used to be able to get up and leave if they started, but you can't anymore.

In your last several telephone conversations with your son, you asked him to "get you out." He has arranged to transport you tomorrow, your eightieth birthday, by air ambulance to his home. He is about to arrive. Neither you nor he has told your wife or daughter about this plan.

Wife/Mother: You are the 76-year-old wife of a man who will be 80 tomorrow. You have been married for fifty-four years. During these years, you have cleaned, cooked, cared for your own two children and your daughter's two sons, and protected your home and family from outsiders.

Just over two months ago, your husband was hospitalized after he was unable to walk. The prostate cancer he was treated for two years ago has spread throughout his body, and at the urging of your son, you and your husband agreed to hospice care for the time he had left. He came home to die. When he came home, all these hospice strangers came into your home and asked thousands of rude, nosy questions about things that were none of their business. Since then, you and your daughter, who calls you several times each day and visits every day, have been able to tell most of them not to come back because you don't need them prying into your business. Now only the nurse comes about once a week.

"That old man," as you call your husband, wants you to do everything for him. You have to take care of him all the time. If he is really dying, how can he be so strong and demanding? Maybe he *can* walk.

Daughter: You are the 47-year-old daughter of a man whose cancer has spread throughout his body. He can no longer walk or take care of the house or car. He decided to come home from the hospital and, at the urging of your brother who lives in another city, enrolled in hospice.

Your parents have always been close by and have been there to take care of you and your two children when things were difficult. Your father has also helped your husband take care of your house and car. You talk to your mother on the telephone often during the day and usually visit every day.

When this hospice stuff started, all these strange people came into the house where you grew up—your house. They upset your mother. They were prying into private matters you wouldn't ever ask your parents. Certainly they were going to send outrageous bills that would use all your parents' savings, and then if the money ran out, they would probably run out too.

Your mother is tired and upset. You and she have to be there all the time. You have to do everything for your father. You have to wait for him to die and leave you.

Son: You are the 45-year-old son of a man who will be 80 tomorrow, the day you will bring him to your home to die. You used to play golf together and fix things around the house together and repair the cars together. A little over two months ago, you went to visit your father when he found out that there was no further treatment for his cancer and he had only a short time left to live. You were there to make arrangements and take care of everything so he could get hospice care for the short time he had left to live. You had a couple of nights after he got home when you talked to one another as you never had before. You felt good when you left. You had said your goodbye to your dad. For you it was over except for the death itself and the funeral. You knew you would probably never see him or talk to him like this again.

Over the past couple of months, you have listened to his tale of desperation and deterioration, wondering if it could really be that bad. Last month when your wife returned from a visit to your father, she confirmed that things were difficult and getting worse.

The hospice office has been in regular contact expressing frustration and increasing difficulty in attempting to provide services. They are clearly going to terminate services shortly since they are being denied entry into your parents' home. In telephone conversations with your father over the past couple of weeks, he has begged to be taken somewhere else.

You and your wife have offered to move him to your home so that he can continued hospice care in your city. You have asked him over and over if he is sure he wants to come because it will mean he can't go back home again. You have arranged for an air ambulance for the next day so you can move him to your home; arranged to get all medical records from doctors, hospital, and hospice; arranged for admission to a local hospice; and are about to arrive at your childhood home and transport your father to your home to live until he dies. Both you and your father have agreed not to tell your mother or your sister what you are doing until you get there. You are now on the street where they live.

Situation 2: Infant Death Decision

Mother/Wife: You are a 33-year-old woman who delivered her third child at home fifteen days ago. Your pregnancy had been difficult and the baby was born prematurely, at twenty-four weeks. It all happened so fast. You had been passing clots and were saving them to be analyzed. You thought you were passing a clot, but it was the baby. You thought you would just hold him for a moment until he died, but he began making little noises, just like a kitten, so you cleared his mouth and called your husband while you tried to keep the baby warm. He was moving and breathing on his own. Your husband called the emergency number, and the paramedics came quickly. They seemed startled to see such a tiny baby. They took the baby from you and took you both to the hospital. Your husband arranged for someone to stay with the other children, who were sleeping. Then he followed you to the hospital. You were admitted, and the baby was moved to the neonatal intensive care unit in a hospital about an hour's drive away.

As soon as he could, you husband drove there to be with the baby. You were released the next day, and have spent most of each day and night with your infant son. He is hooked up to so much equipment. Everything is up and down: sometimes you are sure he will make it, and other times you know he will die. You have told the doctors and the nurses that it is critical that you be with him if he is going to die. They have assured you that you will be notified.

Your other son and your daughter are being cared for by relatives who came to help, but they miss you and your husband because you are away so much. The children have come to the hospital and have been able to see the baby through the window, but they get bored after a short time and want you to leave with them.

In your meetings with the hospital social worker, you have told her that you want your baby to live, and you want everything necessary done to make this possible. You have also told her that you want to be notified if it looks as if your baby might be dying, and if he does, you want to be part of the end of his life. You have also told her that if he dies, you and your husband will transport his body from the hospital to the funeral home in another city.

She was helpful in finding funding resources to help cover the medical expenses, told you that you and your husband would certainly be notified if it looked as if your child were dying, but she also told you that you would not be permitted to leave the hospital with your son's body should he die. She explained to you that it is state law that the body can be released only to a funeral director.

Last night a nurse who had been taking care of your son called you and said it looked as if your son might be dying. Right before she called, you were on the telephone trying to learn about funeral arrangements in case he didn't make it. You found out you could leave the hospital with the body. There was no law prohibiting it.

You and your husband have been at the hospital all night. Early this morning the baby was taken for a CAT scan. The doctor has explained that the baby is probably blind, his leg is badly damaged from treatment, as are his lungs, and that they were able to detect bleeding in the brain. He wants to know what you want to do: continue treatment or have all the equipment that is keeping him alive disconnected.

Father/Husband: You are a 33-year-old doctor who has just opened a medical practice in a small town. Your third child was born fifteen days ago. He was born at home and very premature. You saw him when he was seconds old, and he was moving and breathing on his own. The first doctor you met with at the hospital told you the baby was going to die, but if you wanted, he would have him moved to Children's Hospital, about an hour away. You said you wanted that done. Your wife's doctor said you could ride in the ambulance with the baby, but the paramedics refused. Rather than delay the transfer, you gave up, got in the car, and headed down the road.

It was the middle of the night. You were afraid he would die before you got there. It was hard to leave your wife in the hospital and your other children with strangers, but you knew you needed to go. You kept thinking, "He has to have a name; he can't die without a name." So in spite of the fact that it took you a couple of weeks to name your other children, you decided, on your own, to name him for a great-uncle of yours and your wife's father.

When you got to the hospital, the baby was hooked up to so much life-saving equipment. He was so tiny he would fit in the hollow of your hand. He was still alive, and as the day went on, he got stronger. You had hope that he would live. You arranged to close your office for the day but knew you couldn't do it for long. You were just beginning a practice and heavily in debt from medical school and the new house you just bought and were to move into next week. It was important to be with your son, your wife, and your other children. Somehow you managed.

Most days you worked and then drove the hour to the hospital and back. It was hard not to spend time with your other children, not to manage the move to the new house, which both your and your wife's relatives did for you.

Sometimes you believe your son will live, and other times you know it can't happen. You know that because of the number of times that they have had to put him on 100 percent oxygen that there has probably been eye and lung damage. His leg is almost purple; he will surely lose several toes, if not his whole foot or leg. Those things would be difficult, but you and your family could live with them. This baby has fought hard to live.

Your family is the center of your life. Your choice of medicine as a second career was arrived at so you would have time and money for your family. Here was your youngest son so much in need of a medical miracle, but you knew it was all a juggling act. One thing after another went wrong, and in attempting to correct it, something else would go wrong.

Last night you got a call from the hospital that your son probably was dying. You and your wife wanted to be with him and hold him when he died. You have been able to hold him seldom, but each time you reached into the isolette, he held your finger tightly. He had opened his eyes only once. You were tied together in your helplessness.

Since you got to the hospital last night, your child has been given a CAT scan, and there was evidence of bleeding in the brain. The doctor has asked you and your wife what you want to do now. You want your son to live. His pulse and heartbeat have been strong and steady since he came back from the CAT scan. You have just said to your wife, "Do you really think he's dying?" If he is, you know that you want to be the one to carry him from this hospital and just once, before you bury him, take him to your new house on the hill. You need to decide whether to continue treatment or remove him from the life-saving equipment.

Social Worker: You have been working with a couple in their early thirties whose third child is in the neonatal intensive unit of the hospital in which you work. Your main contact has been with the wife because her husband isn't here when you are. You have helped identify and apply for financial help for the care of their child and spent time trying to prepare her for the probable death of her child. She hangs on to every hope that her child will live, but you have been able to discuss the possibility of his death with her the past few days. In your last conversation, she said if he died, she and her husband wanted to transport his body from the hospital. You had never heard such a thing. You know that the funeral director always picks up the body. You tried to tell her this.

You assured her that she and her husband would be notified if the doctor thought that the baby was going to die, that they would be able to be with their child while he was dying and after he died if they liked, but they would have to release the body to a funeral director. There were just some things that couldn't be done.

Doctor: You are one of a team of doctors who has been caring for a 15-day-old premature male. Try as you have, things have just deteriorated with this child. You can't reproduce the environment of the womb. It looks as if this baby is going to die. Last night you asked the nurse to notify the parents.

They are close to your age, and he is a medical professional. He must know what is happening. They have been insistent that they be notified if the baby is going to die. They want to be with him, which means you will have to be with them when the life-saving equipment is disconnected. They have told the social worker that they want to leave the hospital with the body. You have just gone over the results of this morning's CAT scan, which revealed some bleeding in the brain, and have asked them what they want to do: continue treatment or disconnect the baby from the equipment. They have asked you to leave them alone for a little while so they can talk it over and make a decision. You are waiting for them to make a decision.

Nurse: Last night you had to call the parents of a child you have been caring for since he arrived in your unit fifteen days ago. They have been here much of the time since their child arrived in the neonatal intensive unit. They have brought their other children to the hospital to look through a window at their baby brother. Aunts, grandparents, uncles, and friends have been here with them much of the time also. This child and his family are certainly loved and supported by family and friends. But that isn't going to be enough to keep him alive.

You've seen miracle babies since you've been here, but this isn't going to be one of them. You've helped the parents care for him and made sure they had time to hold him when you were here. You think that in their heart of hearts, they know he won't live, but it is important to them to be with him when he dies, as it has been to be with him while he lived. They want to transport his body after he dies and are getting a hard time about it.

You know the doctor has given them the results of the CAT scan and asked them what they want to do. They have asked that you be with them during many of the procedures. You are about to go off duty for three days. You are quite sure this is the last time you will see them and that by the time you come back to work that the baby will have died, but you've been wrong before. What do you do now?

Situation 3: AIDS and Education

Principal: You are a 40-year-old male who has been the principal of an elementary school for two and a half years in a large urban area. You have worked hard in the school system and have achieved a great deal in the ten years since you came here from a theater career in New York. You are also coowner of and instructor in a local and rather successful dance studio.

Several months ago you were diagnosed as having AIDS. You have been out sick a great deal lately due to the effects of the disease. It's becoming increasingly clear that you won't be able to continue in this job much longer.

You are a good teacher, a good administrator, and a good team leader. You have been able to unify a very diverse staff; you are well liked by the students, staff, and the community. You haven't told anyone at school or in the school system that you have AIDS, although that hasn't stopped rumors.

Your partner has taken over your dance classes and management of the studio. Your energy is at a minimum. Sometimes it seems to take all you have just to get through the day. Being in an elementary school, you are exposed to many opportunities for infection, but you love your job.

You know that eventually you will have to take extended sick leave and probably resign. You have scheduled an appointment with the superintendent of schools to tell him your situation. You would like to keep working as long as you can and hope that this can be worked out.

Superintendent of Schools: The principal of one of the elementary schools in your school system has scheduled a meeting with you for today. You are aware that he has been out sick quite a bit in the past few months.

Earlier in the week you got a call from the PTA president of this school. She was concerned because of rumors in the community that the principal has AIDS. Several parents requested that she call you and express their concern for the health and safety of their children.

Your school system has a nondiscrimination policy regarding AIDS, yet you see a potential problem with the community. This principal has done a remarkable job in both the school and the community and is well liked by the majority of staff, students, and parents. One story in the local paper could do a great deal of damage. If the rumors exist in the community, the newspaper inquiries won't be far behind. You are quite sure about what you are going to hear from this man and wonder what to advise him to do.

PTA President: Several parents have called you with rumors that the principal of the school your child attends has AIDS. Some parents insisted that you call the superintendent and demand that the principal be fired; others were afraid and concerned.

You have worked well with this principal and admire the skill with which he has created a unified staff, an involved community, and eager, happy students. Your daughter has never been happier in school and is doing well academically after a rocky start.

Although you felt uncomfortable doing so, you called the superintendent and expressed the concern of the other parents. You debated going directly to the principal and even attempted to do so several times, but he was out sick.

Today your daughter came home in tears and said a classmate told her that the principal has AIDS, that he is going to die, and the children might also get it and die. What do you say to her?

Fifth-Grade Student: You used to hate school. Everybody was fighting and mad all the time, but a couple of years ago you got a new principal. He was happy all the time, and there were plays and dancing and singing, and school work was fun—and you learned too. People didn't seem to be mad and fight anymore. You liked him, and he seemed to like everybody—even people you couldn't stand.

He hasn't been in school a lot lately. Today at recess, a classmate told you he heard his parents talking; they said that the principal had AIDS and he was going to die—and you might, too, because he was in the school, and you would catch it from him.

You wanted to tell your classmate it wasn't true, but you didn't know, and just last week you heard your mother talking to someone on the telephone about AIDS and rumors and the principal. You are mad, and sad, and afraid. You rush home from school and ask your mother about it. You're sure she will tell you it's all a mistake.

Situation 4: Euthanasia and Hospice

Hospice Patient: You are a 56-year-old female who has been a hospice patient for 5 months. During this time, your husband and your sister have been your primary caregivers. You haven't died, and you haven't gotten better. Earlier this week, something happened, and you can no longer talk or move. You can hear how tired your husband and your sister are. They have been keeping a constant vigil with you. You can't talk or move or let them know in any way that you can hear and understand them. You are tired, and every movement is painful. You wish you could tell them when the pain starts so they would give you the morphine when you need it. They administer it on a schedule, and it isn't enough. When will this end? What would you like to tell them?

Husband: Your wife has been a hospice patient for five months. You and her sister are her primary caregivers. The hospice staff, volunteers, family, and friends have been an incredible help. Without them, you wouldn't have been able to do this.

You have been married for twelve years, and it is a second marriage for each of you. It has been a good marriage for the most part—a comfortable marriage. When she fell ill, and it was clear she would die soon, you decided a hospice was the best solution. Her sister who lives nearby volunteered to help you with her care. So far both of you have been able to stay on your jobs with the help of hospice volunteers and hired medical help.

Last week something happened, probably a heart attack or a stroke, and your wife has not been able to communicate or even open her eyes. Although she is probably in a coma, you continue to talk to her and care for her. The only response you have gotten is when you have had to move her. There is no sound, but her eyes open and her face is contorted as if in a silent scream. The pain must be terrible. If only you knew when and what caused the pain, you could control it. Right now you are just giving the shots on a schedule—guessing if it's time.

When this happened, it seemed as if she would die very soon. You haven't been to work for a week. You have been sitting with her as much of the time as possible. Your sister-in-law has continued to work but has taken a couple of days off to spell you so you can get some sleep. Both of you are beyond tired.

Neither one of you can continue to do this. As you sit with your wife, you tell her how much you love her, how tired you are, how it hurts to see her in pain, how it's time to let go. You know this has to end. You are scheduled to give her a morphine shot and wonder what you are going to do.

Sister: You have been one of your sister's two primary caregivers. She has been a hospice patient for five months. When this began, you decided that you could do this for your sister and her husband. Her first marriage had been a mistake, and these past twelve years had been good. There were ups and downs, but basically she and her husband had been happy and had welcomed you into their lives. This is a gift you could give them.

Until last week, it really hadn't been difficult, once you rearranged your life and your mind. This was the end of your time with your sister. Most people aren't lucky enough to have this kind of time to say goodbye to the people they love.

You had talked with your sister and her husband about what she wanted if things got out of control or difficult or she wasn't responding. She wanted to live as long as she was able to respond and participate in life but not after that— not when her soul or spirit were gone.

You haven't gotten much sleep this past week, and although you had gone to work on and off, your concentration was gone. You would come home, sit with your sister, help your brother-in-law, talk, try to stay awake. This dying was so long. You are each taking two-hour shifts—sleep, sit, sleep. You are so tired.

To you it seems that her life is gone. Her only response this week has been horrible grimaces of pain; she can no longer speak. The morphine doesn't seem to be making a difference. She is gone except for the pain. Maybe this is the time to do something. It's what she said she wanted.

Situation 5: Desired Death

Mother/Wife: Your husband is dead. You have wished him dead so long and so many times that you can hardly believe it's true. You are afraid he will walk back in that front door, drunk and screaming, demanding sex, and if you refuse he will get a gun or knife out. So much of your energy has been used up just trying to get through each day, you hardly have any left to be glad he's dead and you didn't do it. You just want to go to sleep . . . a sleep where you won't have to be watchful for your own or your children's safety.

He was driving home from his job as a security officer, his fifteenth job as a security officer. He loved jobs where he could carry a gun, and though he couldn't keep the jobs very long, he kept being hired. He probably had a six-pack of beer while he was working and another on his way home.

While he was driving home, he must have been so drunk that he drove right into the back of a parked truck and was killed instantly. No bail money this time, no promises, no begging, no blaming you for what happened, no more having to listen to your family tell you how rotten your husband is, no more having to explain to your children why.

For so long you thought you could change him—you could help him be better, keep a job, stop abusing you and the children, stop drinking. But in the last year, you have realized that you are the one who is going to have to change and find a way out of this life. You found a part-time job and were planning to go back to school so you could get a better job. You weren't sure how you would ever do it because it was so hard to just get through each day alive and protect your children. Now he is gone.

You have to make funeral arrangements and have no insurance and no money for next month's rent, let alone for a funeral. You have to tell your children and your family what's happened. You have three children. Two are his boys from a previous marriage. They are teenagers and following many of their father's behaviors. Your other child is a daughter who is 9 and loved her father and desperately wanted his love. No matter what he did, she forgave him and tried to please him.

The children will be awake soon. What will you tell them, your family, and his mother? How will you arrange a funeral? Where will you find the money to bury this man you came to hate more than love?

Daughter: You are 9 years old. You heard someone come to the door in the middle of the night. There was quiet talking and then nothing. Your father was probably arrested again, and your mother was trying to figure out if there was anyone she could call for bail money. At least he didn't come home drunk and wild.

You love your father and wish you could be good enough so he would love you too. Sometimes he was happy and played with you, but mostly he talked about who he was going to sue or kill, or he would get drunk and talk about how sexy other women were and call your mother a pig.

You wish your family was like other families. Your two brothers are always picking on you, and one of them has started to hit you really hard when he is mad or drunk.

You could tell your mother was up, and she would probably be mad again because Dad got arrested. She was always threatening to leave him in jail.

You knew it was time to get up and get ready for school.

Son: You are 15 but look older because you are so big. You were out late last night drinking with some guys you hang around with. You tried to hot-wire a car but ran when someone yelled out a window.

When you heard someone come to the door last night, you listened while the police told your mother that your father had been killed when he drove into the back of a truck. You thought they were coming about you. You have been awake since then thinking about what his death means.

You hate your dad and have threatened to kill him lately when you were angry or when he tried to hit you. It was mostly when he was drunk. He would call you a bastard. When you were younger, he used to shave your head when he got really mad at you.

The woman you called your mother wasn't really your mother.

She had married your father when you were 4. Before that you lived with your grandmother. You can't remember your real mother and have never seen or heard from her. She left your dad when you were 1 or 2 years old, and neither you nor your brother has ever heard from her since.

You wonder what will happen to you now. Your brother is asleep. Maybe you should wake him up and tell him what has happened. Pretty soon it will be time to get up and go to school.

Situation 6: Suicide

Daughter/Sister: Your brother died yesterday. They say it was an accident, but you have found a notebook he had been keeping for a long time. You have been reading for several hours and now believe that this was not an accident but a suicide that he had been planning for a long time. You had no idea he was so miserable until you read this.

You have been away at college for two years. When you left, he had just started tenth grade. You have seen him only when you have been home on vacation. You don't know many of his friends.

This was the beginning of his senior year in high school. Your parents were proud of him. He was a good student and sure to get a scholarship to the college he wanted to attend. He was also active in sports and several other groups at school. Every time you called home, they had another story of what he was doing.

Your father is so sad he is crying all the time, and your mother is in a daze—like a robot going through all the motions. They console one another by saying his death was an accident and that there was nothing that they could have done to prevent it. You now think differently.

Tonight there will be a wake and a funeral tomorrow. You wonder what will be gained by showing them what you have found. What will it do to them? Yet how can you keep it to yourself?

You decide to call your old English teacher who had been your brother's English teacher this year and last year. Keeping a notebook had always been an assignment in that class. You wonder if she had read this notebook too. She had always given you good advice and maybe could help you with this problem.

You have arranged to meet her at the school at the end of the day. As you walk in, you see your brother's picture in the trophy cabinet draped in black cloth with a sign, "We love you and will never forget you." You stare at it and listen to several students who are standing nearby discussing your brother and how well they knew him. You wonder. As you walk down the hall, a teacher who never had time for you when you were there grabs you and hugs you and says, "Oh honey, what a terrible thing to happen to all of us. God must have other plans for him. You'll be OK once you get back to school." Then she rushes on down the hall.

You get to the classroom, and when you open the door, there is your brother's girlfriend and the English teacher.

Teacher: Yesterday a student of yours died in an accident. At least you hope it was an accident. You had this boy in honors English last year also and his sister several years ago. He was funny, insightful, gifted, and hard working, but also there was a dark, mysterious, sad side that surfaced in his writing, especially in the notebook you have students keep.

Several times you had tried to discuss with him what he had written in the notebook. But he joked about it and assured you it was nothing to worry about. Shortly after your last conversation about his notebook, he handed in a brand new one and said that he had lost the old one. It sat on your desk ready to return to him.

Earlier today his sister had called and asked if she could come over and talk to you this afternoon. All day you have been with students who are grappling with his death and the reality of their own mortality. About five minutes ago, his girlfriend, who is not one of your students, came in and accused you of killing him because he told you what he was going to do in his notebooks and you didn't do anything about it. His sister has just opened the door and in her hand you see the first notebook, the one he said he lost.

Girlfriend: Yesterday the boy you have been going out with since last spring, when you asked him to the prom, died. You both had jobs and went away during the summer, so you only saw each other every couple of weeks. You were looking forward to more time together now that you were both back in school full time.

Everyone thinks his death was an accident, but you are sure it was suicide. Two or three times he had let you read a notebook he kept for English class. The things you read scared you so much that you couldn't talk to him about them. He tried to bring them up several times, but you joked with him, and he seemed to feel better. Anyway, if he was writing this for his English teacher, she would do something about it. She would know what to do; you sure didn't.

Now he was dead because she didn't do anything. You didn't know his family very well, so it was hard to go to them. You didn't know what you would say if you did. You had met his sister once last summer when she was home for a short vacation. His parents were really nice, but what could you say to them?

You have told two of your friends that you think he committed suicide and that the English teacher knew he was going to do it. They encouraged you to go to the teacher and talk about it.

Right after school, you went to her room and told her you thought she killed your boyfriend because she knew what he was going to do and didn't stop him. You see his notebook on her desk and start to sob.

You can't talk. She has asked you to sit down, and just as you do, the door opens, and there is his sister. She is carrying a notebook that looks just like the one on the desk.

Situation 7: Restructured Family

Mother: Your son, the doctor, died this morning while he was jogging. His first wife and his second wife are meeting to plan the funeral and have called to ask you if you and your husband would like to help them. This is such a crazy world.

Both you and your husband are practicing Jews; your son was not, although on the high holy days, he brought his sons to your house to celebrate with the family. Their mother, his first wife, was a Protestant, and his current wife is a Catholic. This is sure to be some hodgepodge of a funeral.

After talking with your husband, you decide to meet with the wives and make sure your son's Jewish heritage is part of this funeral. You and your husband are on your way to his house to meet with them now. You have called your other son and your rabbi and asked them to stand by if you need their help.

Father of Wife 1: Your daughter called about an hour ago. Her first husband, your grandchildren's father, died early this morning while jogging. He was supposed to pick up the boys for the weekend in a few hours, and they didn't know their father had died yet. The eleven year old was at the pool, and the sixteen year old was at work. Her current husband had gone to get them and tell them.

Meanwhile your daughter was going to her ex-husband's house to meet with his current wife and his parents to plan the funeral. You have always been the one to take charge when someone in your family died. You know how to make the arrangements and take care of everything. Although the boys were raised "kind-of Jewish," their father was not a practicing Jew, and when your daughter and her ex-husband were married, they celebrated Christmas and Easter with you. The boys and their mother and her husband still do, so they are "kind of Christian" too. You are sure you could arrange the funeral in your church without too much trouble.

Your daughter has asked you to drive her to the house where she and her ex-husband's second wife are meeting to plan the funeral. You are ready to organize the funeral when you get there.

He was a great guy and a good father to your grandchildren. Both he and your daughter are happily remarried. You see his parents with the kids from time to time or at the grocery store, and you are all on good terms. You are glad you will be able to help.

Wife 1: You got a call a few hours ago from your former husband's wife. He died of a heart attack while jogging that morning. You are stunned. You had just talked to him yesterday about picking up the kids today.

You have both remarried, and any of the discomfort of the divorce is long gone. You like his wife, and he and your husband got along well. In working together on how to best care for the boys, you worked as four parents rather than two with separate mates. In the process, you also came to be friends to one another. In a strange way, his death makes you a widow of sorts.

His second wife has asked if you would help her plan the funeral. She has also asked his parents to join you. You have never planned a funeral before. In your family, your father always knew what to do, and everyone called him. You called him to let him know about the death and ask him to drive you to the house.

Your husband has taken the car and gone to get the boys and tell them about their father. They are expecting to be picked up to spend the weekend with him. You are torn: should you go to the meeting or find the boys and tell them yourself? Your husband assured you he would find them, tell them, and then bring them to their father's home so you could all be together.

You and your father are almost there. He has been talking a lot as you drive, but you haven't heard what he has been saying because you are preoccupied. You will be glad to see these people who are your family and will be glad when your husband gets there with the boys. They were close to their father and will miss him so much. You are worried about them.

Wife 2:   You have been married for four years to a man who is a doctor and a hospital administrator. Both of you have good careers and jobs that demand a great deal of your time and energy. Your husband had two children from his first marriage, and rather than have any children of your own, you have worked very closely with him and his first wife and her current husband to make these children your own. The children spend time with you every week, and your husband was to pick them up this afternoon after work.

This morning your husband went out to job as usual, and you left for work before he returned. When you got to work, there was a message to go to the emergency room at the hospital where he worked. You thought perhaps he sprained his ankle and needed a ride home. You would probably have to leave work early to pick up the boys for the weekend. You grabbed some work in case you had to wait for him in the emergency room. When you got there, they told you he had had a heart attack while jogging and had died before anyone found him.

When you got home, you called his former wife, the boys' mother, and his parents and asked them to help you plan the funeral. These people are his family too and should be part of this. Your family lives in another city and will be arriving tomorrow or later, depending on the funeral arrangements you make.

Although both you and your husband were brought up with religion as a central part of your lives, you are not practicing members of any religious group now. Your family is Catholic and his Jewish, and you celebrate religious holidays with both your families more as family holidays than as religious expressions.

Perhaps an interdenominational service at the hospital where he worked would be best. You have called the hospital to see if this is possible in the next few days.

You will be glad when everyone gets here and you can plan the funeral for this man, whom you loved so much, with the others who also loved him so much.

5 Artistic Considerations

THIS is not truly a new category of fully outlined SLEs, but the manual would not be complete without mention of the many media sources that are useful for reflecting on life and death. We believe that good literature and media sources with death-and-loss themes offer the best death education material; it provides the context and the richness of variety that only the growing number of sources of materials at all developmental levels can now afford.

Works of fiction, plays, essays, poetry, films, music, videos, and art hold special opportunities for rich learning and powerful contemplation and identification by the reader, listener, or audience. Loss and death, universal and unique, and the occasion of reflection, creation, and evaluation are powerful themes in the arts.

It is often in reflection and examination of these creative works that we are able to come to terms with our own lives and losses and contemplate our own and others' deaths. Many excellent works lend themselves marvelously to reflective learning experience in death education. Readers are encouraged to investigate available sources and to devise ways to compare such works or to use them in facilitating attitude formation with students.

The field of death education has grown steadily; there are numerous helpful publications with which to augment classroom or workshop experiences. Although it is not the intent of this book to catalog these, we strongly recommend a careful selection from among them as primary reading material for learning more about the contemporary matters of living in the face of human mortality.

This chapter presents a generic approach to death education through the arts—written, fine, and performing. Many of the questions raised in this chapter will apply to a variety of situations. We invite you to choose from among them when and where they are an appropriate vehicle to facilitate death education in the context of the teachable moment.

Examining the Vision

Goals

1. To explore our feelings and attitudes toward death and dying in relation to literature, films, music, and other artistic avenues.
2. To examine others' viewpoints and reactions to death, dying, grief, and bereavement as presented in their creative expressions.
3. To include rather than avoid death when it is presented in the context of an artistic work.

Materials

Any artistic expression that has death as part of its context.

Time

Will vary from piece to piece and group to group, depending on the context of the discussion.

Procedure

The procedure will vary depending on the occasion that invites this discussion. It could be a classroom, workshop, or discussion after a movie or concert or following a bedtime story. Discussing death in the context of presentation is the key; questions are a guide.

Variations

This activity can become more structured by assigning specific works to provide a common experience with death issues as the deliberate focus or by asking participants to bring in an artistic creation that expresses a specific attitude toward death in life.

Debriefing

The following list of questions that a facilitator may wish to draw from is not meant to be exhaustive, all inclusive, or limiting in any way. It is meant to generate ideas that may be included in the context of any discussion of an artistic work that deals with death as an issue or an event. Sometimes only one or two questions are appropriate; sometimes more are. We need not avoid death as an issue but include it in context and contemplate others' visions of both life and death.

1. Did you like this artwork? Why or why not?
2. Who died?
3. Who or what occasioned or caused the death in this piece?
4. How did you feel when the death occurred?
5. How did others in the work feel when the death occurred?
6. Were there different responses to the death? What were they?
7. How does the death presented and the responses to it fit into your experience?
8. What happened after the death?

9. Do you identify with anyone in this piece? Why or how?
10. Was this death culturally or historically unique?
11. Can you compare it to another death in this piece or another work?
12. How was this death different from others?
13. If death in this work is the result of a deliberate action, what motivated this action?
14. Was the motivation sufficient? Why or why not?
15. How are love and hate and life and death connected in this place?
16. How does the impending or recent death of a family member affect the different members of the family and the family as a whole?
17. What role did family members play in supporting one another? What roles did friends play?
18. Was mental health or mental illness a factor?
19. Did institutions have a role in the death, grief, or bereavement presented? If so, was this a positive or a negative role?
20. What different age groups were represented? What was the reaction of each? Do you consider this an age appropriate reaction?
21. Were (are) symbols part of the presentation? What were they? What did they represent? Were they effective?
22. Was anyone responsible for the death? What was the reaction to that responsibility?
23. What were the survivors' responses to the death?
24. How do your beliefs and feelings compare with those presented in the piece?
25. Did you notice conflicting responses or reactions to death?
26. Has this exercise presented any new ideas for your consideration?
27. If you were to create a piece to express your attitude toward life and death, what medium would you choose? What would your message be?
28. Is entertainment a form of death education?

6 Multisession SLE: Grief

THE final activity in this book is a formated multisession group experience. Its focus is on assisting bereaved people with some similar features to get further along with their grief work. This activity has been used for over a decade by one of the authors to accomplish this purpose. It is not to be engaged in lightly or led by one uninitiated in both group dynamics and grief theory. It can be a highly useful adjunct to facilitating the development of more satisfactory coping resources for the bereaved. The structure given here is more akin to the latticework on which to support the burden of growth than to an exacting recipe for merely enduring or attempting to cast off one's mourning needs. Several hundred people have benefited from using it prudently. We hope it will foster the same outcomes for other appropriate users.

Resolving Personal Loss*

Goals

This is a multisession structured learning experience for a group of similarly bereaved individuals to assist them in finding a means of furthering their grief work. As such, it is a model for a modified self-help program and is not intended to be a substitute for counseling or therapy. There are four specific goals of the group experience:

*Adapted from Drum, D.J. and Knott, J.E. *Structured groups for facilitating development* (New York: Human Science Press, 1977), pp. 261–272. Reprinted with permission.

1. To assist the bereaved in recognizing their loss.
2. To further necessary grief work.
3. To create an acceptable mourning rite.
4. To enable the bereaved to begin resuming satisfactory living in the absence of the dead person.

Materials

A comfortable room with flexible (circular) seating arrangements, plus a board or newsprint to write on.

Time

Five weekly meetings of 2 hours each. Each session focuses on a sequence of topics common to the bereaved. Resolution of these issues is felt to be a priority for satisfactory grieving.

Procedure

The targeted group for this program are people who have lost a relationship important to them due to death. In order to determine who is best suited to participate in this structured group, a screening interview is held with each prospective member. Criteria for inclusion are a combination of recency of loss and relationship to the decedent. Members of the family and other intimately related survivors may be ready for such grief work only after the passage of a month or so following the death. Persons with ties not so close in relationship do not appear to need this period to be psychologically open and prepared for the group. The composition of the group should not reflect too much variance from these guidelines and should be somewhat homogeneous with respect to the criteria. Membership should be limited to a maximum of eight; if a coleader is used, a dozen is the recommended limit.

The outline that follows is a session-by-session format.

Session 1

1. Convene the group by asking each member to take a turn stating his or her name and answering these three items by way of self-introduction:

   - Why I am here.
   - What I hope to gain.
   - Who has died.

   It is usually easier to break the ice slowly by having members pair up to do this introduction initially for about 10 minutes before asking them to discuss their response aloud. (30–40 minutes)
2. A welcome to all. Proceed to describe the stated goals of the program. Give an overview of the five sessions and answer any questions posed. (10 minutes)
3. Offer some commentary covering the types of changes members might expect, including somatic and psychic manifestations of grief. Encourage the members to share their feelings as candidly as comfort allows and to discuss the impact of their particular death

loss. Unlike many other group experiences, they are encouraged to talk about their feelings between sessions with nonmembers, particularly with others who knew the dead person. Such objectives as "grief shared is grief diminished" and giving "permission" to detach oneself from all but the memory of the dead are facilitated in this manner. In the first meeting, these issues are openly discussed. (remainder of the session)

Session 2

Begin this session by addressing some of the most typical rections of persons bereaved by the death of someone cherished. Asking each member to react briefly to such experiences as feelings triggered by key words like *loneliness, anger, guilt,* and *deprivation.* As each is said, participants are asked to respond to the emotions the words evoke. Later topics for discussion in this session may include both the physical reaction alluded to in the first session and economic situations consequent to the loss.

Through this activity, group members are given the opportunity to identify their primary grief reactions and begin to own them. Thus there are several objectives: for members to see the legitimacy and commonality of having such emotional responses to their death loss; to provide the leader (and the rest of the group) with a picture of the range and intensity of these issues for this particular group (they usually vary somewhat); and to gain information so that this and the next two sessions can be organized about the more demanding concerns of the members. Other aspects of coping with death loss that come up at this time include the consequences of stigma (social treatment of the bereaved by uneasy sympathizers) and the notion of transition itself, including the goals of detachment and reintegration—all prime needs, which are frequently stated. (full session)

This is a good point at which to give the members some homework, beginning with a voluntary exchange of telephone numbers among those who desire. The purpose is to enable them to check with each other between sessions. Too often the recently bereaved undergo leper-like social treatment by people normally close to them; the concern demonstrated by one person's attending to another with as little as a periodic telephone call can be a powerful element in helping to resolve grief. This is often the case when death is relatively recent and is especially useful if the death resulted in someone's being widowed.

Session 3

1. Begin with a general inquiry about the homework and members' contacts since the last session, plus any notable occurrences a group member may wish to share. (20 minutes maximum)
2. Then focus attention on a topic not covered in the previous ses-

sion's debriefing: anger and guilt feelings are most often the dominant concerns at this juncture in the group's life. In talking openly about such conflicting and (to them) supposedly inimical feelings, members ventilate their feelings and, it is hoped, gain some perspective on understanding them. (1 hour)

3. This last portion of the meeting is devoted to a lecture by the leader on normal grief reactions and on time as a key variable in the mourning process. Often issues such as keeping up with the daily demands of living in the face of immobilizing depression, the ambiguity of the future, and strained or absent social activity are teased out and discussed at some length in this session. This discussion is intended to help bereaved members pursue their grief work. (remainder of the meeting)

Session 4

During this session, the focus is on stigma and the social distance and relative isolation that the death of a person confers on anguished survivors. The effects of deprivation—both social and economic—are also dealt with at this session. Personal fears of vulnerability and mortality, especially such fears as "cancer contagion" or hereditary defects, should also be dealt with openly in this meeting if they have not surfaced before. These are common fears yet will vary from group to group. Also, in this meeting, and to a lesser extent in the previous one, the leader may find it useful to employ some rational contradiction. Disputation of seemingly irrational fears, while not always consoling, will usually make an impact on a bereaved person over time.

This is also the session in which the group begins to bridge the gap from being centered on the past (dead) to focusing on the present (the living self and others) and ultimately to planning for the future. One way to facilitate this transition is to use a device like the Gestalt "empty chair" technique for "saying goodbye" to the dead person(s), usually with one member who has evinced difficulty in affirming the death as real. This has the purpose of helping members to confirm aloud the death thereby gain some semblance of psychological closure on that episode.

The homework assignment for the final session requires members to return the following week with some well-considered strategies for dealing with their day-to-day needs and wants in the light of the major changes incurred by the death loss. Usually it is best to have members write down these strategies for sharing at the next meeting.

Session 5

1. To begin this final meeting, members form themselves into groups of two to four persons each, the exact composition to be of their own making. Within these small groups, each individual shares his or her plans, and the other member(s) offer supportive critique, suggestions, and encouragement. (about 30 minutes)

2. The leader reconvenes the total group and solicits reactions to the discussions held in the subgroups. (15–20 minutes)
3. After briefly processing those, the leader recapitulates the process of the group, soliciting members' comments. He or she urges individuals to recognize and affirm their change process to date and their growing abilities to adjust to life in the face of death and to note other gains made in the course of the five weeks, including new friends and resources. This serves as a summary debriefing for the previous four sessions as well. (25 minutes)
4. Finally, the predictable matter of separation anxiety needs to be dealt with. It has been found useful to respond to this need by asking each member to speak briefly about what the group has meant personally, citing specific highlights. This activity concludes the group experience itself. (30 minutes)

The objectives of this session are to make the transition from group to self as the major resource in the grieving process and to enable participants to gain reinforcement for their strategies and goals for satisfactory survival.

Debriefing

Throughout each session, there are built-in opportunities for processing the activities. That is, in fact, the core dynamic of this SLE. Members should have the opportunity to offer both written and oral feedback about the total experience at the conclusion of the last session—on paper with a systematic approach or by participants writing an open-ended set of comments about the high and low points, as well as what helped and what was not so useful. Thereby, the activities can be fine-tuned for subsequent offerings.

Index

About the Authors

J. Eugene Knott, is a counseling psychologist, administrator, and faculty member at the University of Rhode Island and a former president of the Association for Death Education and Counseling.

Mary C. Ribar, whose graduate work was in family studies, has been chairperson of English and interdisciplinary team leader and has taught English and social studies in Montgomery County, Maryland, public schools, where she is currently employed.

Betty M. Duson is a clinical psychologist who has taught and counseled at the university level. She is currently in private practice in Houston, Texas.

Marc R. King is a clinical psychologist who has counseled and taught in higher education, worked with hospital patients, and currently is in private practice in Dallas, Texas.